Character Before Chords

The Heart of the True Worshipper

Gerard Assey

Character Before Chords:
The Heart of the True Worshipper
By
Gerard Assey

Published by:
Gerard Assey
19/18, Palli Arasan Street
Anna Nagar East
Chennai - 600 102

ISBN: 978-81-993017-9-5

Table of Contents

Preface

There was a time in my life when I thought worship was about sound — the right chord progression, the perfect vocal blend, the energy of the moment. I thought the louder the music and the greater the response, the deeper the worship.

But I was wrong.

Over the years, through both mountaintop moments and valley seasons, the Lord began to peel away the layers of performance and show me something sacred:

Worship is not an art form — it's a heart form.

It isn't about how high we can sing, but how low we are willing to bow. It isn't about who sees us on the platform, but who we are when no one else is looking.

Worship, in its truest form, is not measured by applause but by alignment — the alignment of a human heart with the heart of God.

This book: **"Character Before Chords: *The Heart of the True Worshipper*"**, was birthed from that revelation — a journey of returning to the essence of worship. It is not a manual on music, nor a guide to leading songs, but a call to live a life that pleases the Lord.

As I wrote these chapters, I wasn't trying to create another "how-to" book for worship teams or leaders. I was writing to the person who, deep inside, knows that God is calling them to more — to purity over performance, to humility over hype, to devotion over display.

I've met so many worshippers over the years — some whose talent was extraordinary, yet whose hearts had grown weary or proud; and others whose skill was simple, but whose intimacy with God was breathtaking. It is the latter who truly carry the fragrance of heaven.

This book is for them — and for you.

A Call Back to the Heart

You'll find within these pages stories from Scripture — David in the fields, Mary with her alabaster jar, Moses in the tent, Isaiah in the temple — and each one points to a God who looks beyond the outward act to the inward posture.

You'll also encounter fictional stories inspired by real moments — ordinary men and women who learned that the truest songs are born not from talent, but from tears; not from microphones, but from moments alone with God.

My prayer is that as you read, the Holy Spirit will whisper to your soul and reignite something fresh within you — a longing to know Him more deeply, to worship Him more purely, and to serve Him more humbly.

The Journey Ahead

Each chapter builds on the one before — beginning with the heart's foundation and leading all the way to the overflow of a life transformed by worship.

You'll move from the inner altar (where intimacy and purity are built) to the outer impact (where worship begins to transform others). Along the way, you'll be challenged to examine motives, surrender pride, cultivate humility, and rediscover the joy of simply being in His presence.

You'll be reminded that worship is not just something we *do* — it's who we *become.*

My Personal Prayer for You

As you turn these pages, I invite you to pause often. Let the Scriptures soak in. Let the stories stir reflection. Let the Holy Spirit do heart surgery where needed.

And if at any point you find yourself saying, "Lord, this is me — I've been striving more than surrendering, performing more than pursuing," just stop and lift your heart again before Him. That's where worship begins — right there, in honest surrender.

Because before we hold a mic, we must hold our heart before Him.

Before we sing our songs, we must let Him write His song upon us.

To Every Worshipper

This book is for every worshipper — whether you lead thousands on a platform or quietly sing to Him while doing the dishes. He sees both the same.

The goal is not perfection, but posture — a life that continually bows before the Lord in love, gratitude, and obedience.

My desire is simple: That by the time you close this book, your definition of worship would forever change. That you would understand that God is not after your *song,* He is after your *soul.* And that you would join heaven's chorus not just with your lips, but with your life.

A Final Word Before We Begin

When David wrote, *"Search me, O God, and know my heart"* (Psalm 139:23), he wasn't afraid of what God would find — he was inviting transformation.

May that same prayer become yours as you journey through these pages. Let every chapter become an altar. Let every reflection become an offering. Let every conviction become a song.

And when you reach the end, may your worship have gone deeper — from chords to character, from songs to surrender, from performance to presence.

"For the eyes of the Lord range throughout the earth to strengthen those whose hearts are fully committed to Him." — *2 Chronicles 16:9*

May yours be one of those hearts!

Beyond the Stage — Worship that Touches Heaven

Worship has never been about music. It has always been about the heart. Before there were instruments, microphones, lights, or worship sets, there was a garden — a place where God walked with man in perfect communion. That was worship. It wasn't orchestrated; it was intimate. It wasn't performed; it was lived. When sin entered, it didn't just break man's moral standing with God — it broke his worship. Ever since then, God has been seeking to restore what was lost — not just a sound, but a *relationship*.

Jesus summarized this pursuit in John 4:23–24, when He told the Samaritan woman, *"The hour is coming, and now is, when the true worshippers shall worship the Father in spirit and in truth: for the Father seeketh such to worship Him."* Imagine that — the God who created all things is *seeking* something. He's not seeking songs, systems, or stages. He's seeking *hearts* that are surrendered, authentic, and true.

Over the years, worship has unfortunately become synonymous with music, yet music is only one small vehicle of expression. Worship existed long before music did. Worship is obedience when no one is watching. It is love expressed through faithfulness, even when the feelings fade. It is purity that chooses God over applause. It is tears at His feet when the world demands you stand tall. Worship is not the lifting of hands before people, but the bending of knees before God.

Mary of Bethany — The Worshipper Who Chose Intimacy Over Activity

Few people capture this truth better than Mary of Bethany. **In** Luke 10:38–42, while her sister Martha rushed about preparing and serving, Mary simply sat at Jesus' feet, listening to His words. Martha was doing good things — she was serving the Lord. But Mary was doing the *best* thing — she was *being* with the Lord.

When Martha complained, Jesus gently corrected her: *"Martha, Martha, you are worried and troubled about many things. But one thing is needed, and Mary has chosen that good part, which will not be taken away from her."*

Mary's act wasn't laziness; it was discernment. She recognized that the Lord of glory desired her presence more than her performance. She understood that worship is not about being busy for God but being still *before* God.

Many of us, like Martha, get caught up doing things *for* God, forgetting that He first called us *to* Himself. Mary teaches us that the heart of worship begins in stillness, in attentiveness to His voice, and in giving Him our undivided affection.

David — The Shepherd Whose Heart Sang Before His Harp Did

Long before David held a harp in the courts of Saul, he was singing unseen songs to God under the stars of Bethlehem. As a young shepherd, alone with the sheep, he wrote psalms not for fame but for fellowship. His worship was raw, intimate, and unfiltered. When God later said in 1 Samuel 13:14, *"I have found David son of Jesse, a man after My own*

heart," it wasn't because David was flawless. It was because his worship was *authentic*.
In the quiet of the fields, David learned what many never discover — that the audience of one is enough. That's why when he finally stood before Goliath, he didn't come with armor or titles; he came with the confidence of someone who already knew God in the secret place.
David's story teaches us that worship is forged in obscurity. The songs that please heaven are written not under spotlights but under the shadow of God's presence.

A Tale of Two Worshippers — Applause vs. Altar

Ethan was a gifted young worship leader. His voice was powerful, his style captivating. Crowds would lift their hands, and many admired his anointing. Yet over time, the applause became louder in his ears than the whisper of God. He began to measure success by the size of the crowd rather than the size of his surrender. The more visible he became, the more distant his heart grew from the One he once sang for.
In the same congregation was *Grace*, a quiet intercessor who sat at the back every Sunday. Few noticed her, but heaven did. While others practiced setlists, she prayed over the sanctuary, the worship team, and the people who would walk in. She would often come early and stay late, unseen, whispering simple prayers: *"Lord, let Your presence be felt."* She wasn't on stage, but she was at the altar — daily.
When the church went through a dry season, Ethan felt spiritually empty and creatively drained. But something remarkable happened. In one service, as the atmosphere felt heavy, Grace quietly began to

weep and pray in her seat. Without fanfare, the Spirit of God began to move across the room. Hearts softened. Tears flowed. People began to worship deeply — not because of the music, but because heaven responded to the fragrance of a *heart* that touched God.

Ethan later said, *"That day, I realized something. God never called me to perform worship; He called me to be a worshipper."*

A Call Back to the Heart

This book is written for worshippers like Ethan — and like you and me — who sometimes lose sight of the essence of worship in the noise of ministry, music, and modernity. It's a call to return to the altar, to the simplicity of devotion.

Worship that touches heaven is born from the heart, not from harmony. It flows from intimacy, not industry. It is found in those who, like Mary, choose His presence above all else; like David, worship when no one is watching; and like Grace, pray when no one applauds.

This is what Jesus meant when He said the Father is *seeking* true worshippers. Not perfect voices, not flawless performances — but pure hearts. The Father is not searching for songs that sound good, but for lives that *smell good* — the aroma of love, surrender, and truth rising before His throne.

When worship becomes about applause, it loses its fragrance. But when it's about adoration, it gains eternity.

So before you hold a microphone, hold your heart before Him. Before you rehearse your next song, rehearse your surrender. And before you lead others in worship, make sure you have knelt at His feet like Mary, lingered like David, and prayed like Grace. Because the worship that truly touches heaven always begins with the heart that has been touched by Him.

Scripture Reflection

"The sacrifices of God are a broken spirit; a broken and a contrite heart, O God, You will not despise." — Psalm 51:17

"This people honors Me with their lips, but their heart is far from Me." — Matthew 15:8

Heart Reflection

- ✓ *Is my worship born from love or from routine?*
- ✓ *Do I spend more time preparing my songs or preparing my soul?*
- ✓ *Would I still worship if no one ever saw me do it?*

A Worshipper's Prayer

Lord, draw me back to the heart of worship — to the place where it's all about You. Strip away every pretense, every pride, every performance. Teach me to value Your presence more than platforms. May my worship rise from a heart that is humble, pure, and wholly Yours. Let my songs be sincere, my service be sacred, and my spirit be surrendered. In Jesus' Name, Amen.

Worship Begins in the Heart, Not on the Stage

Before a hand is lifted, a chord is struck, or a song is sung, worship has already begun — deep within the heart. True worship doesn't start when the music starts; it begins in the unseen chambers of our inner life. It is not the rhythm of drums that heaven listens for, but the rhythm of the heart that beats in reverence toward its Maker.

When God sent Samuel to anoint a new king over Israel, the prophet expected someone tall, impressive, and stately — someone who looked the part. But God's words to Samuel in 1 Samuel 16:7 shattered human expectations: *"Do not consider his appearance or his height, for I have rejected him. The Lord does not look at the things people look at. People look at the outward appearance, but the Lord looks at the heart."*

That single verse redefines worship. God is never moved by the outward — He looks deeper. He listens beyond melodies and microphones to motives and meditations. He seeks the *why* behind the *what.*

The Shepherd Who Sang to the Sky

Before David was Israel's greatest psalmist and king, he was a shepherd — anonymous, unseen, and forgotten even by his own family. While his brothers stood before Samuel, David was tending sheep in the quiet hills of Bethlehem. Yet it was there, away from crowds and ceremonies, that his heart learned the language of worship.

We can imagine the young shepherd sitting beneath a canopy of stars, strumming his harp as the night wind whispered through the grass. His songs weren't rehearsed for performance; they were confessions of love. They weren't crafted to impress anyone; they were born out of intimacy with God. Out in those lonely fields, David found an audience of One.

Those were not wasted years — they were *forming years*. When no one saw him, God did. When no one heard his voice, heaven did. When others dismissed him, God was preparing him. So, when the moment came for public anointing, God could say confidently, *"I have found David, a man after My own heart."*

What made David a man after God's heart wasn't his harp, his skill, or his songs. It was the purity and authenticity of his devotion. Before he ever held a crown, he held a heart of worship. Before he stood before people, he knelt before God.

That's where worship truly begins — not in public applause, but in private affection.

The Woman Who Worshipped Through Her Tears

Centuries later, another heart of worship would be revealed in an unlikely place — not in the temple, but in a Pharisee's house. A woman, known in town for her sinful past, entered uninvited. The room grew quiet. The respectable guests shifted uncomfortably. But she didn't care. Her eyes were fixed on Jesus.

Luke 7:37–38 tells the story: *"A woman in that town who lived a sinful life learned that Jesus was eating at the Pharisee's house, so she came there with an alabaster jar of perfume. As she stood behind Him at His feet weeping, she began to wet His feet with her tears. Then she wiped them with her hair, kissed them and poured perfume on them."*

There were no instruments, no microphones, no lyrics — only tears and surrender. Every drop that fell from her eyes was a lyric from her heart. Every breath was a declaration: *"You are worthy of my everything."*

While the Pharisee judged her actions, Jesus saw her heart. He turned to Simon and said, *"Do you see this woman? … her many sins have been forgiven — as her great love has shown"* (Luke 7:44–47).

Her worship broke cultural norms and personal pride. She brought what was costly — not just perfume, but herself. That's what true worship does. It is costly, raw, and deeply personal. It's not always beautiful to those watching, but it's always beautiful to God.

That woman had no platform, but she had a posture that pleased heaven.

When the Stage Replaces the Secret Place

There's a danger in our time — the danger of confusing performance with presence. It's easy to prepare our *setlists* and forget to prepare our *souls.* It's easy to chase excellence on stage but neglect intimacy in the secret place.

No one starts out wanting to perform for people; most begin with sincere love for God. But over time, applause can become addictive. Recognition can replace reverence. The stage that was meant to serve can slowly become the center.

That's what happened to *Lucas,* a young worship leader in a thriving city church. Lucas was talented, passionate, and creative. He knew how to move a crowd. Sunday after Sunday, people complimented his voice, his energy, his music. He started enjoying the spotlight more than the secret place.

In time, his prayer life faded. His rehearsals increased, but his worship diminished. He was still leading songs, but not from overflow — from emptiness. One evening after service, he sat alone in the sanctuary. The lights were dim, the sound system silent. He whispered a prayer he hadn't prayed in months: *"Lord, I don't feel You anymore."*

And in that quiet, the Lord's response came, not in thunder but in conviction: *"You've sung to Me from the stage, but you've stopped being with Me in the secret place."*

That moment broke him. Lucas wept, not out of shame, but out of longing. He realized that what God desired most was not his song but his surrender. From that day on, Lucas began spending time with God privately again — no instruments, no audience. Just stillness. Just prayer. And slowly, joy returned. His worship on stage began to carry a new weight — not because of better sound, but because it once again came from a heart that had been in His presence.

Purity Before Performance

Psalm 51:10–17 captures the cry of a heart that understands this truth. After his failure with Bathsheba, David prayed, *"Create in me a clean heart, O God, and renew a right spirit within me."* He realized that God wasn't after sacrifices or burnt offerings — those could be empty rituals. He said in verse 17, *"The sacrifices of God are a broken spirit; a broken and contrite heart, O God, You will not despise."*

In other words, God measures *purity before performance*. He values repentance over routine, authenticity over activity, and humility over hype.

That means our greatest preparation for worship is not a rehearsal but repentance. It is not about perfecting harmonies but about purifying hearts. God delights in the sound that rises from a surrendered spirit more than any perfectly tuned note.

Seen by Heaven, Known by God

At the end of the day, the question that defines every worshipper is simple:

Am I worshipping to be seen by men, or known by God?

Jesus warned in Matthew 6:1–6 about those who do their acts of devotion to be noticed. He said, *"Your Father, who sees what is done in secret, will reward you."* Heaven notices what the world ignores.

You might not have a stage, a microphone, or a crowd. But if you have a heart that loves Him, you have everything God desires. The quiet worship offered in your living room, the whispered prayer on your way to work, the song you hum through your tears — these are the moments that move His heart the most.

Worship that begins in the heart will always find its way to the stage — but worship that begins on the stage may never reach His heart.

Reflection

When no one sees you, God does. When no one applauds you, heaven still listens.

True worship isn't a performance; it's a posture — a continual turning of the heart toward God.

So, pause for a moment.

Ask yourself:

- ✓ *Is my worship a display or a devotion?*
- ✓ *Have I built a platform while neglecting an altar?*
- ✓ *Would I still sing if no one ever heard my song?*

Because at the end of it all, the Father isn't searching for performers. He's searching for *worshippers* — those whose hearts are His stage.

A Worshipper's Prayer

Lord, teach me to worship You from the inside out. Create in me a clean heart and renew a steadfast spirit within me. Let my secret life overflow into my public life. May my worship be born not from skill but from surrender, not from applause but from adoration. Help me to love Your presence more than any platform, and to seek Your face more than any following. May my life itself become a song that pleases You. In Jesus' name, Amen.

The Private Altar Before the Public Platform

Every public act of worship that carries true power is born in the secret place.

Long before a worshipper stands before people, he or she must first kneel before God. The strength and authority that radiate on the platform are never manufactured under stage lights—they are birthed in the dim glow of a private altar where only God is audience.

Jesus described this sacred rhythm in Matthew 6:6: *"But when you pray, go into your room, close the door and pray to your Father, who is unseen. Then your Father, who sees what is done in secret, will reward you."*

The Father's reward is not fame or visibility—it is His presence. The worshipper who learns to love the secret place receives what no stage can give: intimacy. And intimacy is what gives authenticity to our worship.

Abraham: Building Altars Before Building His Name

From the very beginning, God taught His people to build altars—places of encounter, remembrance, and surrender. One man who understood this deeply was Abraham. Every time God spoke to him or led him somewhere new, Abraham responded the same way: he built an altar.

In Genesis 12:7–8, when God promised to give him the land of Canaan, Abraham's first response was to build an altar and call on the name of the Lord. Later, when he faced trials, when he prospered, and even when he was tested to lay down Isaac, the altar was always central. The altar was his meeting place, his declaration: “God, You are first.”

Abraham never built altars for public admiration—he built them out of private devotion. Long before he became known as the father of many nations, he was first a man who knew how to worship in solitude. His influence was not the result of his wealth or strength, but of his relationship with God in secret.

Every altar he built represented surrender, dependence, and trust. In those moments, Abraham wasn’t performing—he was communing. It was in private altars that his public legacy was shaped.

Moses: The Man Who Met God Face to Face

If Abraham’s life shows us the pattern of building altars, Moses’ life reveals the power of maintaining one. In Exodus 33:7–11, we read that Moses took a tent and pitched it outside the camp, calling it “the Tent of Meeting.” There, “the Lord would speak to Moses face to face, as one speaks to a friend.”

While the people stood at a distance, Moses would go into the tent, and the pillar of cloud would descend. That private encounter changed everything. It was in that secret meeting that Moses received instructions, interceded for his people, and encountered the glory that would later radiate from his face.

Publicly, Moses led a nation out of Egypt; privately, he met with God. His authority before Pharaoh was birthed in the presence of God before the burning bush. His confidence to stretch his rod over the Red Sea came not from technique, but from trust developed in countless quiet moments with the Almighty.

Moses' life reminds every worshipper: if you want to stand before men, you must first learn to kneel before God.

Jesus: Withdrawing to the Father

Even the Son of God modeled this rhythm of retreat. Though multitudes followed Him and the demands of ministry pressed constantly, Jesus often withdrew to lonely places to pray. Luke 5:16 records it simply: *"But Jesus often withdrew to lonely places and prayed."*

It's striking that the one who was God incarnate still prioritized time alone with the Father. Before calling the twelve apostles (Luke 6:12), before performing miracles, before facing the cross—Jesus withdrew.

Those moments of solitude weren't escapes; they were encounters. They were His private altars—places where He replenished His strength, aligned His will, and renewed His heart.

If Jesus needed private communion to fulfill His public calling, how much more do we? The secret place is where perspective is restored, motives are purified, and hearts are filled again with love for the Father.

Nathaniel: The Worshipper Whose Fragrance Filled the Room

Nathaniel was not the most talented musician in his church. His voice was pleasant but ordinary. He didn't have the flair or the charisma that drew attention. Yet, every time he led worship, something different filled the room. There was a depth, a tenderness, an almost tangible fragrance of God's presence that made people weep without understanding why.

Few knew Nathaniel's secret. Every morning, before dawn, he would sit on the edge of his bed with his guitar, not to practice, but to *worship*. There, in the quiet of his small apartment, he would sing simple songs—not to an audience, but to his Friend. Some mornings he sang; other mornings he wept. Sometimes he sat in silence, overwhelmed by the nearness of God.

One Sunday, as the church prepared for a major worship event, the lead singer fell ill. The team reluctantly asked Nathaniel to step in. Nervous but obedient, he walked to the platform. He whispered a quiet prayer: "Lord, this isn't about me. This is for You."

As the first chord sounded, something changed in the atmosphere. People began to lift their hands, tears streaming down their faces. There was no dramatic lighting, no powerful beat—just an unmistakable sense of God's presence. Later that day, one of the elders said softly, "Today, heaven sang with us."

Nathaniel knew why. What the people felt that morning wasn't his talent—it was his altar. His private worship had overflowed into a public moment. His unseen devotion had become the fragrance that shifted an entire room.

Public Authority Flows from Private Intimacy

This is the divine order: intimacy before influence, altar before platform. Many today long for public anointing without private abiding. But authority in worship doesn't come from microphones, music degrees, or ministry titles—it comes from knowing God personally and deeply.

When we spend time with Him in secret, His fragrance clings to us. Like Moses, when we come out of the Tent of Meeting, our faces shine. Like Jesus, when we emerge from prayer, power follows us. Like Nathaniel, when we stand before people, something unseen flows through us—because we've already been with Him.

The private altar is not glamorous. It's often lonely. It's where we confront ourselves, wrestle with our motives, and learn to love God for who He is, not for what He gives. But that is where transformation happens. That's where hearts are made whole, where pride dies, and where worship becomes pure.

Guarding the Secret Place

We live in a noisy, busy world. The temptation is constant—to replace time with God for time on stage, to trade prayer for preparation. But the worshipper's greatest danger is not burnout; it's *distance*.

If the flame of private devotion ever dies, the light on the platform will soon dim. So, build your altar daily. It doesn't need to be elaborate. It may be a corner in your room, a quiet walk in the park, or a few still moments before the day begins. What matters is that it's consistent—and that your heart meets His.

God doesn't need perfect words. He desires honest ones. He's not impressed by long prayers but moved by longing hearts. The private altar is not about ritual; it's about relationship.

A Heart's Reflection

When you stand before people, what they see is only the fruit. The roots lie in what happens when no one is watching.

Ask yourself:

- ✓ *Do I have a private altar, or only a public platform?*
- ✓ *Do I meet with God because I love Him, or because I need Him to bless my ministry?*
- ✓ *When was the last time I worshipped without a song, without a microphone—just me and Him?*

Remember, the anointing that moves hearts publicly is birthed in the secret place privately.

A Worshipper's Prayer

Father, teach me to love the secret place more than the stage. Let my heart burn for Your presence when no one is watching. Forgive me for the times I've substituted public ministry for private communion. Build in me an altar of devotion—a place where I meet You daily, where pride is laid down and intimacy is restored. May my public worship always be the overflow of private intimacy. Let my songs rise from a heart that has been with You, and let every chord carry the fragrance of Your presence. In Jesus' name, Amen.

The Posture of Humility — Bowing Low to Lift Him High

There is no posture more powerful in worship than humility. It is not a musical posture, but a heart one. It's the quiet bending of the soul before a holy God — a recognition that *He is everything, and we are nothing without Him.* Worship is not about elevating ourselves; it is about lowering ourselves before the One who alone is worthy to be lifted high.

Pride is subtle. It doesn't always wear arrogance on its sleeve. Sometimes it dresses in talent, hides behind ministry, and smiles through confidence. It can even disguise itself in worship — when the applause of men begins to mean more than the approval of God. But true worship and pride can never coexist. The moment pride enters, the fragrance leaves.

The Apostle Paul painted a clear picture of the ultimate example of humility in Philippians 2:5–11: *"Let this mind be in you, which was also in Christ Jesus: who, being in very nature God, did not consider equality with God something to be used to His own advantage; rather, He made Himself nothing by taking the very nature of a servant, being made in human likeness. And being found in appearance as a man, He humbled Himself by becoming obedient to death—even death on a cross."*

If the Son of God chose humility as His posture of worship, how much more should we? Jesus' entire life was an act of worship — not through songs, but through surrender. He bowed lower than anyone so that the Father could be lifted higher than all.

David's Dance — The Humility That Delights Heaven

Few scenes in Scripture capture humility in worship more vividly than the day King David danced before the Lord. The Ark of the Covenant — the symbol of God's presence — was finally returning to Jerusalem. It was a day of rejoicing. Priests were playing instruments, the people were shouting, and in the middle of it all, David, the king of Israel, was dancing "with all his might" (2 Samuel 6:14).

There were no royal robes that day — David had laid them aside. He wasn't concerned about how he looked; his only concern was how God felt. He wasn't performing for people; he was celebrating before the Presence.

When his wife Michal saw him through the window, she despised him. To her, the king's behavior seemed undignified. Later, she confronted him: *"How the king of Israel distinguished himself today, going around half-naked in full view of the slave girls of his servants as any vulgar fellow would!"*

But David's response reveals his heart: *"It was before the Lord, who chose me rather than your father or anyone from his house… I will celebrate before the Lord. I will become even more undignified than this, and I will be humiliated in my own eyes."*

That's humility. David didn't worship to protect his image; he worshipped to honor God's. He understood that no title, no position, and no crown could ever make him greater than the One who lifted him from tending sheep to leading a nation.

David's humility invited God's presence. Saul's pride had driven it away.

Saul's Pride vs. David's Humility

Saul and David both started with divine calling, but only one ended with divine favor.

When Saul was anointed as king, he began humbly. He even hid among the baggage when Samuel came looking for him (1 Samuel 10:22). But success slowly poisoned his soul. Pride crept in like a quiet shadow. Saul began to care more about what people thought of him than what God commanded.

In 1 Samuel 15, God instructed Saul to completely destroy the Amalekites and everything that belonged to them. But Saul spared the best animals, claiming it was for sacrifice. When Samuel confronted him, Saul justified his disobedience instead of repenting.

Samuel's words still echo today: *"Does the Lord delight in burnt offerings and sacrifices as much as in obeying the Lord? To obey is better than sacrifice, and to heed is better than the fat of rams."* (1 Samuel 15:22)

Saul's worship became polluted by self-importance. He built monuments to himself instead of altars to God. His pride blinded him to the truth that obedience and humility are the essence of worship.

David, in contrast, remained aware of his smallness before God, even at the height of his success. He sinned, yes—but he also repented deeply. His psalms reveal a man who constantly humbled himself before the Lord: *"Create in me a clean heart, O God, and renew a steadfast spirit within me."* (Psalm 51:10)

That's why, despite his failures, David was called *"a man after God's own heart."* Humility was the thread that kept his heart tethered to God's.

Heaven Always Exalts the Humble

James 4:6 reminds us, *"God resists the proud, but gives grace to the humble."* The proud build platforms; the humble build altars. The proud seek attention; the humble seek His presence. And heaven always favors the latter.

Humility is not weakness; it is strength under submission. It's not thinking less of yourself, but thinking of yourself less. It's the willingness to step back so that Jesus can be seen more clearly.

Pride says, *"Look what I've done."* Humility says, *"Look what He has done."*

Pride performs. Humility bows!

Ethan's Story — The Worship Leader Who Bowed Again

Ethan had been a worship leader for almost twenty years. His voice was seasoned, his stage presence confident, and his team respected him. But somewhere along the way, he began to drift. The ministry that once flowed from brokenness had become routine. He didn't realize it, but he had begun to depend more on his experience than on God's presence.

It was a Sunday morning when everything changed. During worship, as the team sang their usual set, something felt… flat. There was no flow, no fire. Ethan sensed it. After service, he went home troubled. Later that evening, he sat alone in his living room and prayed for the first time in months—not a rehearsed prayer, but a real one: *"Lord, what happened? Why does it feel like I'm singing, but You're not near?"*

The answer came softly, almost like a whisper in his spirit: *"You stopped bowing."*

Tears filled his eyes. He realized that though his knees still bent on stage, his heart had been standing tall before God. He had been leading worship but not living worship. That night, Ethan fell on his knees—not before a crowd, but before his King. He repented, he wept, and he worshipped.

Weeks later, when he returned to lead again, something was different. The songs hadn't changed—but the spirit behind them had. The team noticed it. The congregation felt it. The presence of God filled the room again.

Ethan later told his team, *"Worship isn't about how high we can lift our hands; it's about how low we're willing to bow our hearts."*

You Can't Lift God High if You're Still Standing Tall

Pride is like a shadow — it grows the closer you move toward the light, unless you continually bow lower. The moment we start thinking we've "arrived," we stop truly worshipping. The essence of worship is the recognition of our complete dependence on God.

If we wish to lift Him high, we must first bow low. Worship is an invitation to self-forgetfulness — to lose ourselves so that Christ might be magnified. That's what John the Baptist meant when he said, *"He must increase, but I must decrease."* (John 3:30)

When a worshipper bows low, God stands tall. When we humble ourselves under His mighty hand, He lifts us up (1 Peter 5:6). The paradox of worship is that the lower you go, the higher the glory rises.

Reflections from the Secret Place

The posture of humility cannot be faked. It's not about outward gestures of bowing or kneeling; it's about the inward bending of the heart. You may raise your hands in worship while still standing tall in pride. But when the heart bows—truly bows—heaven leans close.

Ask yourself:

✓ *Have I allowed success, skill, or recognition to make me forget who I'm singing for? When was the last time I fell on my knees—not for a need, but for love? Would I still worship if no one ever thanked me, recognized me, or applauded me?*

True worshippers bow low not because they have to, but because they *can't help it.* The nearer they draw to the greatness of God, the smaller they see themselves.

A Worshipper's Prayer

"Lord, teach me the beauty of bowing low. Deliver me from the pride that steals Your presence. Strip away every need to be seen, every desire to be applauded. Let my heart bow before You in reverent love and holy fear. Like David, let me be willing to be "undignified" for Your glory. Like Jesus, help me to empty myself and serve others with joy. May my songs never rise higher than my surrender, and may my posture always say, "You alone are worthy." In Your precious name, Amen".

When we choose humility, we create space for God's presence to dwell. The fragrance of true worship rises from hearts that know their place—not on the throne, but at His feet. For it is there, in the low place, that heaven meets earth, and God is lifted high.

Purity Over Performance — Guarding the Heart of a Worshipper

There's a quiet danger that walks beside every worshipper—especially those who stand in the light of visibility. The greater the stage, the greater the temptation to trade purity for performance, holiness for hype, and presence for popularity.

The world may celebrate the gifted, but heaven crowns the pure. True worship is not measured by the sound that fills a room but by the sanctity that fills a heart.

In Psalm 24:3–4, David asked the most sobering question every worshipper must still ask today: *"Who may ascend the mountain of the Lord? Who may stand in His holy place? The one who has clean hands and a pure heart, who does not trust in an idol or swear by a false god."*

To "ascend" into the presence of God has never been about talent or training; it has always been about purity. You can play skillfully, sing powerfully, and still not stand acceptably before Him if the heart is compromised.

Jesus affirmed the same truth in Matthew 5:8: *"Blessed are the pure in heart, for they shall see God."* Purity is not perfection—it's transparency. It's the refusal to live a double life. It's the courage to keep the inside as clean as the outside.

The Subtle Trade — When Performance Replaces Purity

There's a temptation in ministry to substitute visible success for inner integrity. The stage can easily become a mask that hides the quiet erosion of the soul. One can be applauded by people and yet distant from God.

Performance is easy to measure—it draws attention, it gains followers, it looks impressive. But purity is hidden—it draws no applause, yet it draws heaven's attention.

The truth is, God is not moved by how good we sound; He's moved by how clean we stand.

Joseph: The Man Who Chose the Prison Over Compromise

If there ever was an Old Testament example of purity under pressure, it was Joseph. Sold as a slave, betrayed by his brothers, and forgotten by men, Joseph still kept his heart right before God.

When Potiphar's wife tried to seduce him, Joseph's response in Genesis 39:9 reveals the depth of his purity: *"How then could I do such a wicked thing and sin against God?"*

He could have reasoned, "No one will know," or "I've already suffered enough, I deserve this comfort." But Joseph understood something sacred—sin is not primarily against people; it is against God.

Choosing purity cost him everything. He lost his position, his comfort, and his reputation. But what he gained was far greater: the approval of heaven and the presence of God.

Years later, when Joseph stood before Pharaoh, interpreting dreams and ruling a nation, his integrity was still his crown. The purity he protected in private became the authority God released in public.

Joseph's story reminds every worshipper that *character must come before calling*. Purity is not a burden—it's a blessing. It may not open every earthly door, but it always keeps heaven's door wide open.

Ananias and Sapphira: When Deception Destroys Devotion

The early church was marked by awe, generosity, and the manifest presence of God. Yet, in the midst of revival, two worshippers named Ananias and Sapphira learned a tragic lesson about purity.

In Acts 5, they sold a piece of property and decided to lie about how much they gave, pretending to offer the full amount to the apostles. Their deception wasn't about money—it was about motive. They wanted recognition without sacrifice. They desired reputation without righteousness.

Peter's words cut to the heart of the matter: *"Ananias, why has Satan filled your heart to lie to the Holy Spirit?"* (Acts 5:3)

Their sin wasn't public immorality—it was hidden hypocrisy. They wanted the honor of holiness without the cost of honesty.

The result was devastating. Both fell dead. It seems harsh until we realize the seriousness of the sin. God was establishing a standard in His new church—that purity matters more than performance, and authenticity more than applause.

It is a warning to every generation of worshippers: the Holy Spirit is not impressed by what we pretend to give. He sees not the song we sing, but the heart we bring.

The Story of Leah — When the Applause Fades

Leah was one of the most talented worship singers in her church. Her voice carried emotion, her range was remarkable, and her passion seemed unstoppable. Over time, she began leading worship at conferences, recording songs, and receiving invitations from across the country.

But with recognition came pressure—to always look the part, sound perfect, and maintain the image of success. Gradually, her private life began to drift. Her time with God grew shorter, her conversations shallower, her motives mixed.

Then one night, while preparing for a major concert, she sat at her piano and realized something chilling: she couldn't feel God's presence anymore. She was singing the same songs, but they sounded empty. Her voice was strong, but her spirit was weak.

She knelt down and whispered through tears, *"Lord, where are You?"*

And in that silence, a quiet conviction filled her heart: *"You've been polishing your performance, but neglecting your purity."*

That night became her turning point. Leah canceled her upcoming events, took a sabbatical, and began rebuilding her altar. She stopped singing to crowds for a while and started singing again to Jesus. She repented, she rested, she returned.

Months later, when she finally stood on a platform again, something had changed. The tone of her voice carried brokenness. The songs felt real. People wept, not because of her skill, but because heaven had returned to her sound.

Leah later said, *"Purity brought back what performance stole."*

Excellence Without Holiness Becomes Entertainment

There's nothing wrong with pursuing excellence—God deserves our best. The psalmist even commands, *"Play skillfully, and shout for joy."* (Psalm

33:3) But excellence without holiness is empty. When skill becomes more important than sanctity, worship turns into entertainment.

God is not impressed by perfect harmonies sung from polluted hearts. He delights in imperfect songs offered from sincere hearts. A broken hallelujah from a clean heart moves Him more than a flawless performance from a proud one.

The stage is not the place to showcase skill; it is a place to reveal surrender. Every chord, every lyric, every gesture should flow from a life that has been purified in His presence.

Guarding the Heart — The Worshipper's Lifelong Battle

Purity is not something you achieve once and keep forever. It's a daily pursuit—a constant guarding of the heart. Proverbs 4:23 warns, *"Above all else, guard your heart, for everything you do flows from it."*

As a worshipper, you are constantly exposed to admiration, attention, and influence—all of which can become subtle toxins if not guarded carefully. Temptation doesn't always come as immorality; it sometimes comes as ego, entitlement, or exhaustion.

To guard the heart is to keep your motives pure:

- ✓ *Why am I doing this?*
- ✓ *Who am I really singing for?*
- ✓ *Is my heart still tender toward His presence, or hardened by performance?*

The pure heart keeps worship pure.

The Reward of Purity

The promise of Jesus in Matthew 5:8 is breathtaking: *"Blessed are the pure in heart, for they shall see God."*

That's the reward—*seeing Him.* Experiencing His nearness. Feeling His presence. Living with the awareness that He is pleased. Nothing compares to that. No applause, no award, no audience can ever replace the joy of knowing that God sees your heart and delights in it.

The pure worshipper may not always be the most famous, but they will always be the most fruitful. Their ministry will carry weight, not because of charisma, but because of character. Their songs will carry healing, because they come from hands and hearts that are clean.

A Heart Reflection

You can impress people with performance, but you can only please God with purity.

So pause for a moment and ask:

- ✓ *Have I allowed the applause of people to dilute the holiness of my worship?*
- ✓ *Is there anything hidden in my heart that needs cleansing?*
- ✓ *Would I still serve, still worship, still love Him, even if no one noticed?*

Remember: the purity you protect today determines the power you carry tomorrow.

A Worshipper's Prayer

"Father, search me and know my heart. Expose anything in me that is impure, dishonest, or divided. Teach me to love Your presence more than popularity. Wash my motives, cleanse my mind, and renew my spirit. Let my songs rise from clean hands and a pure heart. Deliver me from the need to perform, and bring me back to the simplicity of worship. May my excellence always flow from

holiness, and my ministry from intimacy. I choose purity over performance, presence over platform, and holiness over hype.
In Jesus' name, Amen."

Purity is not the perfection of life, but the direction of the heart.
When a worshipper lives clean before God, every note becomes sacred, every lyric becomes life, and every moment of worship becomes a meeting place between heaven and earth.
***Because in the end,* God desires clean hands and a pure heart more than polished skills.**

Obedience — The Fragrance That Heaven Smells

There is a fragrance that pleases heaven far more than the sweetest melody or the most skillful harmony — it's the fragrance of obedience. True worship does not begin with a song on our lips, but with a "yes" in our hearts.

Worship without obedience is noise. It might sound beautiful to men, but in the courts of heaven, it is hollow. The truest act of worship is not the lifting of hands, but the laying down of will.

The prophet Samuel said it best in 1 Samuel 15:22: *"Does the Lord delight in burnt offerings and sacrifices as much as in obeying the Lord? To obey is better than sacrifice, and to heed is better than the fat of rams."*

God is not impressed with outward expressions of worship that are disconnected from inward submission. You can sing louder, play better, even serve faithfully — but if the heart refuses to obey, heaven remains unmoved.

Obedience is not about compliance; it is about love. It's our way of saying, "Lord, I trust You more than I trust myself." It's surrender with sound — a melody of submission that rises straight to His throne.

Abraham: When Worship Looked Like Surrender

In **Genesis 22**, we meet a man whose obedience would forever define the meaning of true worship — Abraham.

After years of waiting for the promised son, Isaac was finally born. Abraham's joy was complete. Yet one day, God tested him: *"Take your son, your only son, whom you love — Isaac — and go to the region of Moriah. Sacrifice him there as a burnt offering on a mountain I will show you."* (Genesis 22:2)

The command was unthinkable. Isaac was not just a child — he was the promise. Yet Abraham didn't argue, reason, or delay. Verse 3 simply says, *"Early the next morning Abraham got up and loaded his donkey."*

There were no explanations, no conditions, no bargains. Just obedience.

As they climbed the mountain, Isaac asked, *"Father, the fire and wood are here, but where is the lamb?"* Abraham's reply revealed the heart of a true worshipper: *"God Himself will provide."*

On that mountain, Abraham lifted the knife not in cruelty but in confidence — that the same God who gave the promise was able to fulfill it, even through death. And just before the act, heaven intervened.

"Do not lay a hand on the boy," the angel said. *"Now I know that you fear God."* (Genesis 22:12)

That phrase — "Now I know" — captures the essence of obedience. It's the moment heaven witnesses love that costs something.

Abraham didn't just worship with words; he worshipped with obedience. His surrender released a fragrance that reached the throne of God, and from that day, the Lord swore blessing over him and his descendants forever.

True obedience always brings a response from heaven.

Jesus: The Sound of Perfect Obedience

Centuries later, the Son of God would walk the same path of obedience — but this time, there would be no ram in the thicket.

Philippians 2:8 says, *"He humbled Himself and became obedient to death — even death on a cross."* Jesus' entire life was a song of obedience. From His birth in a manger to His final breath on the cross, every moment was submission to the Father's will. In Gethsemane, when His soul was overwhelmed with sorrow, He prayed, *"Father, if it is possible, let this cup pass from Me. Yet not as I will, but as You will."* (Matthew 26:39)

That prayer — that surrender — was worship in its purest form. There were no instruments, no audience, no applause — only obedience.

And it was through that obedience that salvation was birthed. Heaven's greatest victory came through one man's total surrender.

Obedience always carries resurrection on the other side. When we die to our will, God breathes His life into ours. When we lay something down, He lifts something greater up.

Nathan's Story: The Worship Leader Who Chose to Forgive

Nathan was a respected worship leader in his church. For years, he had served faithfully, mentoring younger musicians, writing songs, and leading the congregation into powerful moments of worship. But one day, everything changed.

During a leadership transition, misunderstandings arose. Words were twisted, motives questioned. In a painful turn of events, Nathan was removed from his position. The decision cut deep — not because of pride, but because of betrayal from those he trusted.

At first, Nathan told himself he was fine. But bitterness quietly began to build. Every time he heard another worship set led by someone else, something twisted inside him. He avoided people. He smiled on the outside, but inside he was hardening.

One evening, as he sat alone strumming his guitar, he heard a whisper in his spirit:

- ✓ *"Will you still worship Me when no one lets you lead?"*
- ✓ *Tears welled up. The words pierced deeper:*
- ✓ *"Will you obey Me, even when they wrong you?"*

He knew what God was asking. Forgive them. Bless them. Let go.

It wasn't easy. Everything in him wanted to explain, defend, justify. But that night, Nathan chose obedience over emotion. He wrote down every name that had hurt him, prayed for them one by one, and said aloud through tears, *"Lord, I release them. I choose to obey You."*

The next morning, something changed. The heaviness that had followed him for months lifted. For the first time in a long time, he felt peace — not the kind that comes from vindication, but the kind that comes from obedience.

Months later, his pastor called unexpectedly. "Nathan, we've been praying," he said, "and we feel the Lord leading us to restore you to leadership."

When Nathan stood on that platform again, he didn't feel the need to prove anything. His worship was deeper now, quieter, purer. It wasn't about position anymore; it was about presence. He later said, *"Forgiveness was my act of worship. It was the hardest song I ever had to sing, but the one heaven heard the loudest."*

Obedience had opened heaven over his life again.

Romans 12:1 — The Worship of a Surrendered Life

Paul summarized the essence of obedience in Romans 12:1: *"Therefore, I urge you, brothers and sisters, in view of God's mercy, to offer your bodies as a living sacrifice, holy and pleasing to God — this is your true and proper worship."*

A living sacrifice is one that stays on the altar even when it's painful, inconvenient, or misunderstood. It's saying "yes" when your flesh screams "no." It's surrendering your plans, your timeline, your pride, your comfort — all because He is worthy.

Obedience is not always glamorous. It sometimes feels costly, lonely, or even unseen. But heaven measures worship not by visibility, but by vulnerability.

Every act of obedience — big or small — releases a fragrance in heaven.

When you forgive, it smells like grace.

When you let go of bitterness, it smells like love.

When you serve without recognition, it smells like humility.

When you obey without understanding, it smells like faith.

That's the aroma that reaches the throne room — the fragrance of a surrendered heart.

The Sound Heaven Hears

We often think of worship as something we offer *upward* — songs rising, hands lifted, instruments playing. But in God's ears, obedience has a sound too. It's the sound of footsteps moving in the direction of His will. It's the sound of hearts saying, "Yes, Lord."

Heaven responds to obedience. It always has. When Abraham obeyed, blessing followed. When Joseph obeyed, favor followed. When Jesus obeyed, salvation followed.
If worship is the song, obedience is the rhythm that keeps it true.

Reflection: The Heart That Says "Yes"
True worship is not proven by what we sing, but by what we do after the song ends.
Ask yourself:

- ✓ *When God asks for something difficult, is my answer still "yes"?*
- ✓ *Do I obey when no one is watching?*
- ✓ *Do I trust His timing even when it disappoints mine?*

Every "yes" strengthens intimacy. Every act of obedience tunes the heart to heaven's frequency.

A Worshipper's Prayer
"Father, teach me the beauty of obedience. Help me to value Your voice above my own understanding. When You speak, let my heart say "yes" without hesitation. I lay down my will, my rights, and my reasoning. I want to worship You not just in song, but in surrender.
Let my obedience rise like incense before You — a fragrance that fills Your throne room with delight. May my life be the song that never stops saying, "Your will be done." In Jesus' name, Amen"

Obedience is heaven's favorite melody. It may not always be heard by crowds, but it's always recognized by God. For while skill moves people, obedience moves heaven — and that's the truest sound of worship there is.

The Hidden Life — Becoming a Worshipper in Secret

There is a kind of worship that never makes it to the stage, yet it fills heaven with fragrance. It is quiet, unseen, uncelebrated, and often unnoticed by men — but it is profoundly noticed by God.

In a world obsessed with visibility, God still treasures the hidden. In a culture that measures worth by likes, followers, and applause, heaven still measures by faithfulness. There's something sacred about a life that seeks no spotlight, a worshipper who doesn't crave recognition, and a heart that delights to be known only by God.

Colossians 3:3 says, *"For you died, and your life is now hidden with Christ in God."* Those words hold a mystery — that the truest life is one hidden in Him. What the world cannot see, heaven celebrates.

Jesus emphasized this principle in Matthew 6:1–6, teaching His followers not to practice their righteousness "to be seen by others." He said, *"When you pray, go into your room, close the door and pray to your Father, who is unseen. Then your Father, who sees what is done in secret, will reward you."*

There it is again — the Father sees what is done in secret.

The hidden life is the secret chamber of every true worshipper — the place where reputation dies and relationship is born. It's the space where no one applauds, yet God draws near; where no one notices, yet heaven takes note.

Elijah at the Brook Cherith — God's Classroom of Isolation

Before Elijah ever stood before kings or called down fire from heaven, he was hidden by a brook.

In 1 Kings 17:2–6, after declaring drought over Israel, God told Elijah, *"Leave here, turn eastward and hide yourself by the brook Cherith, east of the Jordan. You shall drink from the brook, and I have commanded the ravens to feed you there."*

Those words — *"hide yourself"* — were not punishment; they were preparation.

At Cherith, Elijah was stripped of platform, popularity, and even basic comforts. His only company was a stream of water and a few black-feathered waiters bringing his daily bread. Yet it was there, in hiddenness, that he learned dependence.

There was no audience at Cherith, no one to witness his prayers or measure his ministry. But God was watching, shaping him for a greater assignment. Before Elijah could stand on Mount Carmel and call down fire before a nation, he had to learn to kneel in private and call down faith before his God.

Every public demonstration of power must first be preceded by private discipline in obscurity. The hidden seasons are God's classrooms. The brook is where He teaches us that His presence is enough.

When the brook finally dried, Elijah didn't panic — he obeyed. That's the fruit of hidden life: calmness in silence, trust in transition, and obedience in uncertainty.

The hidden life purifies the heart, quiets the ego, and births the kind of worship that endures.

Anna the Prophetess — Faithful in the Shadows

The New Testament gives us another beautiful picture of a hidden worshipper — Anna the prophetess.

In Luke 2:36–38, Anna appears briefly in the nativity story, but her life speaks volumes. A widow for decades, she never left the temple, worshipping night and day with fasting and prayer.

No titles. No platform. No recognition. Just worship.

When Mary and Joseph brought baby Jesus into the temple, Anna was there. She recognized what others missed — the Messiah had come. God revealed Himself not to the prominent priests or temple leaders, but to a woman who had quietly sought Him for years.

Her reward was divine revelation. While others busied themselves with temple duties, Anna saw what heaven was doing. She saw redemption wrapped in swaddling cloth.

This is what happens in hiddenness: revelation comes to those who wait. God reserves His deepest secrets for those who spend time in His presence when no one is watching.

Anna's life whispers a truth that our generation must hear — *the ones who worship faithfully in the shadows often become the first to see the light.*

The Janitor — Worship from the Back Row

Every Sunday morning, before the worship team arrived and before the sanctuary lights came on, Daniel unlocked the church doors. He wasn't a singer or a musician; he was the janitor.

Few noticed him. He wore simple clothes and carried an old ring of keys that jingled softly as he walked through the empty church. But Daniel had a secret.

Before anyone arrived, he would stop by the stage, lay a hand on the instruments, and pray.
"Lord," he would whisper, *"anoint these hands that will play, these voices that will sing, and these hearts that will lead Your people today."*
Sometimes, he would sit quietly in the last row, worshipping long before the first note was struck. His eyes would close, and tears would roll down his cheeks as he whispered thanks for God's faithfulness.
No one saw. No one applauded. No one even knew. But heaven did.
One Sunday, the worship team walked in early and found Daniel praying near the drum set. They stood silently at the door, listening. His prayer wasn't eloquent; it was tender. *"Lord, let Your glory fill this place before they even sing."*
That morning, the service was unlike any other. The atmosphere was charged with God's presence. People wept, repented, and were healed during worship. The pastor later said, "I don't know what changed today, but something shifted."
What they didn't know was that someone had already prepared the atmosphere long before the music began.
When Daniel passed away years later, few in the congregation realized who he really was. But in heaven's records, his name was written among worshippers who changed atmospheres without ever holding a microphone.
He was proof that heaven values hidden faithfulness far above visible fame.

Heaven's Perspective: Hidden but Heard

There's something profoundly freeing about living unseen by men but fully known by God. When your worth isn't tied to applause, you become unshakable. When your joy doesn't depend on recognition, you become unstoppable.

Jesus said in Matthew 6:6, *"Your Father, who sees in secret, will reward you."* That means nothing done in His name, no act of devotion, no whispered prayer, no quiet obedience ever goes unnoticed by Him.

While the world counts numbers, God counts moments — the unseen tears, the private prayers, the small sacrifices made out of love. Those are the moments heaven treasures.

Some of the most anointed worshippers on earth may never release an album, lead a service, or stand before crowds. But their fragrance fills heaven's throne room. They are the unseen pillars upholding the visible.

Every church has its "Daniels" — those who pray behind the scenes, intercede during rehearsals, or worship from the back row. They may never be recognized on earth, but heaven knows their names.

The Gift of Hiddenness

Hiddenness is not punishment; it's protection. God hides you to heal you, to shape you, and to keep your heart pure. If you're in a season where no one notices your effort, where your prayers feel unseen, and your faithfulness feels forgotten, take comfort — you are in Cherith.

God is developing depth before display. He's building roots before revealing fruit.

When the time is right, He will bring you out — but until then, stay hidden in Him. Worship where you are. Serve where you are. Love Him in the shadows, and He will reveal Himself in the light.

Hidden worship is pure worship — because it seeks no audience but One.

Reflection: The Secret That Satisfies

Ask yourself:

- ✓ *Am I content to be unseen by men but fully seen by God?*
- ✓ *Do I worship only when there's recognition, or do I still lift my voice in secret?*
- ✓ *Am I willing to let God hide me, trusting that He is working in the unseen?*

Remember this: what is hidden on earth is often highlighted in heaven.

The fragrance of true worship doesn't need a crowd — it only needs a heart that loves Him in secret.

A Worshipper's Prayer

"Father, thank You for the gift of hiddenness.

Teach me to love the secret place where You see and I am seen by You alone. Forgive me for craving recognition more than relationship. Help me to find joy in serving quietly, faithfully, and unseen. Like Elijah, help me to trust You by the brook. Like Anna, let my worship rise continually, even if no one notices. And like Daniel, may my hidden prayers prepare the ground for Your glory. Let my unseen devotion release a fragrance that fills heaven,

For You are the only audience I need. In Jesus' name, Amen."

In the hidden life, a worshipper discovers the sweetest secret — that the eyes of men may miss you, but the gaze of God never does. And in that quiet knowing, the heart finds its truest song.

Because when no one sees your worship, heaven still smells its fragrance.

Integrity in Worship — Living What You Sing

There's something beautiful about a song that is sung from a sincere heart. But there's something even more powerful about a life that sings what the lips declare. True worship is not only what we *sing* before God; it is what we *live* before men.

Integrity is the harmony between what we say and what we do, between what we proclaim in the sanctuary and how we behave outside it. A worshipper without integrity is like an instrument out of tune — it may still produce sound, but the melody is off.

The psalmist asked in Psalm 15:1–2, *"Lord, who may dwell in Your sacred tent? Who may live on Your holy mountain? The one whose walk is blameless, who does what is righteous, who speaks the truth from their heart."*

Notice that David didn't say, "The one who sings beautifully" or "The one who plays skillfully." He said, "The one whose walk is blameless." God measures worship not by the volume of our songs but by the integrity of our steps.

Jesus echoed this in Matthew 15:8, saying, *"These people honor Me with their lips, but their hearts are far from Me."*

Those are sobering words. They remind us that God doesn't listen to lyrics; He listens to lives.

Daniel: Integrity in Captivity

If ever there was a man who worshipped through consistency rather than convenience, it was Daniel.

Taken captive from his homeland and thrust into the pagan culture of Babylon, Daniel could have easily compromised. He was young, talented, and in the king's service — every opportunity to blend in was available. Yet, from the beginning, Daniel drew a line. In Daniel 1:8, it says, *"But Daniel resolved not to defile himself with the royal food and wine."*

That decision may seem small, but it was massive in meaning. The king's table represented indulgence, comfort, and compromise. Daniel's refusal wasn't about diet — it was about devotion. His integrity wasn't situational; it was spiritual.

Years later, when jealous officials tried to destroy him, they couldn't find a single fault. So they attacked his faith, knowing that the only thing Daniel would never compromise was his worship.

In Daniel 6:10, even after a decree was issued forbidding prayer, we read, *"Now when Daniel learned that the decree had been published, he went home to his upstairs room where the windows opened toward Jerusalem. Three times a day he got down on his knees and prayed, giving thanks to his God, just as he had done before."*

Those words — *"just as he had done before"* — reveal the essence of integrity. Daniel's worship didn't change with circumstance. Whether in freedom or captivity, in favor or danger, his devotion remained the same.

His worship wasn't an act of performance but of principle. The man who prayed in secret was the same man who stood in public.

God honored that consistency. When Daniel was thrown into the lions' den, heaven sent angels to shut the lions' mouths. Because integrity always attracts divine protection.

Daniel teaches us that real worship isn't proven when we're on stage — it's proven when we're in Babylon.

Peter: From Failure to Faithfulness

In the New Testament, few people embody the struggle between words and actions like **Peter**. He loved Jesus deeply, but his passion sometimes outpaced his integrity.

The night Jesus was arrested, Peter swore, *"Even if everyone else deserts You, I never will."* (Matthew 26:33) Yet only hours later, he denied even knowing Jesus — not once, but three times.

When the rooster crowed, Peter remembered the Lord's words and wept bitterly. Those tears weren't just sorrow; they were the beginning of restoration.

After His resurrection, Jesus appeared to Peter by the Sea of Galilee. In John 21:15–17, we read that Jesus asked him three times, *"Simon, son of John, do you love Me?"*

Each time, Peter answered, "Yes, Lord, You know that I love You." And each time, Jesus replied, *"Feed My sheep."*

Notice what Jesus did: He didn't ask Peter to sing louder, serve harder, or prove himself on stage. He called him to live differently — to let his love show in his life.

That is integrity — when repentance becomes restoration and failure turns into faithfulness. From that day, Peter's life matched his confession. The man who once denied Jesus stood boldly in Acts 2, proclaiming Him before thousands. His words now carried weight because his heart carried truth.

Integrity gave authority to Peter's worship. The same voice that once said, "I don't know Him," now declared, "There is no other name under heaven given to men by which we must be saved."

When Lyrics and Life Collide

It's easy to sing *"I surrender all"* while still holding on to control, to declare "I will follow You" yet walk our own way, to cry "You alone are worthy" yet crave human approval.

Integrity challenges us to close the gap between our lyrics and our lifestyle. It asks, *"Do I mean what I sing?"* and *"Does my Monday reflect my Sunday?"*

When the heart and the hands don't agree, worship loses its purity.

Integrity isn't about perfection — it's about honesty. It's not pretending to have it all together; it's choosing to be real with God and people.

The most powerful worship is consistency — being the same person offstage as on it.

The Story of Caleb — When Integrity Became a Song

Caleb was a talented keyboardist in his church. His skill was undeniable, and people often told him he could "feel" the music in his soul. He loved leading worship, but over time, small cracks began to appear in his character.

He started arriving late for rehearsals, dismissing corrections, and quietly criticizing others behind their backs. His attitude on stage was joyful, but off stage, it was often prideful.

One day, after a tense rehearsal, his worship pastor pulled him aside and said gently, *"Caleb, your playing is beautiful, but your heart is drifting. Remember, worship is not about what your hands can do — it's about who your heart belongs to."*

That night, Caleb couldn't sleep. He sat in his room, replaying his own words from Sunday: *"Lord, I give You my heart."* Suddenly, the lyrics felt heavy. He realized he had been singing lies with truth on his lips.

He fell to his knees and whispered, *"Lord, forgive me. I don't want to just sing right; I want to live right."*

From that day, something changed. Caleb became more intentional — more humble, more accountable, more real. His excellence improved, but this time it flowed from integrity, not ego. And slowly, people began to notice a different kind of anointing — not in his fingers, but in his spirit.

He later told a young musician, *"I learned that the truest chord in worship is the one struck between the heart and the life."*

God's Measure of Worship

Heaven measures worship not by pitch but by purity, not by rhythm but by righteousness.

When David prayed, *"May the words of my mouth and the meditation of my heart be pleasing in Your sight,"* (Psalm 19:14) he was asking for alignment — for the inside and the outside to sound the same.

Integrity is when what you sing on Sunday matches how you live on Saturday. It's when your love for God isn't just lyrical — it's lived.

We cannot lead others into worship we don't live ourselves. The world doesn't need perfect singers; it needs honest ones. Worship loses power when our lives contradict our lyrics, but it becomes unstoppable when our words and walk agree.

Reflection: "Do My Actions Echo My Anthems?"

- ✓ *Every song you sing writes a statement of faith. The question is — are you living it?*
- ✓ *When you sing "Christ be magnified," do you magnify Him in your relationships?*
- ✓ *When you declare "You can have it all, Lord," do you still withhold forgiveness or control?*
- ✓ *When you cry "Nothing else will do," do you still run after lesser things?*

Ask yourself daily:

- ✓ *"Do my actions echo my anthems?"*

Because the greatest sound of worship isn't heard in the sanctuary — it's seen in the life that follows.

A Worshipper's Prayer

"Father, I don't want my songs to outshine my life. Teach me to worship You with integrity — in my words, my actions, and my decisions. Forgive me for the times I've sung what I haven't lived.
Align my heart with my lyrics, and make me the same person in private that I am in public.
Like Daniel, help me to remain faithful no matter the cost.
Like Peter, restore me where I've failed and make my love authentic again.
Let my worship rise not from performance, but from truth.
May my actions always echo my anthems.
In Jesus' name, Amen."

Integrity is the invisible chord that ties the heart of a worshipper to the heart of God. When what we sing and what we live finally sound the same, heaven leans close — because in that harmony, God hears Himself.

The Spirit of Unity — One Sound, One Heart

There is a sound that heaven cannot ignore — the sound of a people united in spirit, heart, and purpose. It is the sound of true worship that rises not from a single voice, but from many hearts beating as one.

When God hears *that* sound, He responds. His glory fills the place. His presence rests upon His people. Because unity has always been the atmosphere where God loves to dwell.

The psalmist declared,

"Behold, how good and pleasant it is when brethren dwell together in unity! It is like the precious oil poured on the head, running down on the beard, on Aaron's beard, down upon the collar of his robe. It is as if the dew of Hermon were falling on Mount Zion. For there the Lord bestows His blessing, even life forevermore." — Psalm 133:1–3

Unity is more than agreement; it's alignment. It's when hearts move in rhythm with heaven and with each other.

Jesus prayed for this very thing in John 17:21, saying, *"That they may all be one, Father, just as You are in Me and I am in You."*

For Jesus, unity wasn't optional — it was essential. He knew that the strength of His body would depend on the harmony of its members.

But unity isn't easy. It requires humility, grace, and a willingness to lay down pride and preference for a greater purpose. It calls us to tune our hearts like instruments — until every string vibrates with the same frequency of love.

The Trumpeters and Singers — One Sound that Brought the Glory

One of the most beautiful pictures of unity in the Old Testament is found during the dedication of Solomon's temple.

In 2 Chronicles 5:13–14, Scripture records,

"The trumpeters and singers joined in unison, as with one voice, to give praise and thanks to the Lord. Accompanied by trumpets, cymbals, and other instruments, they raised their voices in praise to the Lord and sang: 'He is good; His love endures forever.'

Then the temple of the Lord was filled with a cloud, and the priests could not perform their service because of the cloud, for the glory of the Lord filled the temple of God."

Notice the sequence — *when they became one, the glory came.*

The glory didn't fall when the music was perfect or when the instruments were skillfully tuned. It came when the people were united — when the sound was single, when their hearts were synchronized in worship.

God wasn't responding to the melody — He was responding to the unity.

It wasn't their skill that drew His presence; it was their spirit.

The temple was filled not just with music, but with oneness. And heaven filled what earth had harmonized.

That's the secret: unity attracts the glory of God.

The Church in Acts — One Accord, Many Tongues

Centuries later, that same divine pattern reappeared.

In Acts 2:1, we read, *"When the day of Pentecost came, they were all together in one accord in one place."*

That phrase — *"one accord"* — comes from the Greek word *homothymadon*, meaning *"to rush along in unity."* It paints the image of different notes played together to form a single, harmonious sound.

And what happened when they gathered like that?

"Suddenly, a sound like the blowing of a violent wind came from heaven and filled the whole house where they were sitting." (Acts 2:2)

Once again, unity released the sound of heaven.

One accord brought one outpouring.

The Holy Spirit didn't descend upon scattered individuals; He filled a united body. They had different personalities, backgrounds, and stories — yet their focus was singular: *to wait on the promise of the Father.*

The result? A global awakening. The early church was born, and the world was never the same again.

A Worship Team Torn and Restored

At Grace Chapel, the worship team was known for its sound — polished, dynamic, and musically excellent. But behind the smiles and harmonies, cracks were beginning to show.

Ego had quietly slipped in.

One vocalist, Rachel, often felt overlooked because she wasn't given enough solos. The drummer, Aaron, grew resentful that no one recognized the hours he spent rehearsing. The worship leader, Joel, was exhausted trying to manage personalities instead of nurturing presence.

Rehearsals became tense. Conversations turned cold. People showed up out of duty, not devotion.

And though the music still sounded good, something felt missing. The atmosphere was dry — the anointing, faint.

One evening, after another strained rehearsal, Joel gathered the team. His voice trembled as he spoke.

"Friends, we've lost our focus. We've been chasing perfection instead of presence. We sound great together, but we don't love each other anymore. And if we don't love one another, how can we lead others to love God?"

Silence filled the room. Tears began to fall.

That night, they didn't rehearse a single song. Instead, they formed a circle and prayed — really prayed. One by one, team members confessed pride, jealousy, and hurt. Rachel apologized for her attitude. Aaron admitted he had been critical. Joel repented for trying to control outcomes instead of surrendering them.

Something shifted in that circle. The weight that had hung over them lifted. They laughed, hugged, and sang softly together — *"He is good; His love endures forever."*

The following Sunday, when they led worship, the atmosphere was different. The congregation could sense it — the music carried warmth, authenticity, and love. Tears flowed freely. People lingered in God's presence long after the final chord.

Later, Joel said, *"We didn't change our setlist. We changed our spirit."*

And heaven responded.

Because unity isn't a sound we produce — it's a posture we live.

When Heaven Hears One Heart

Unity doesn't mean sameness; it means selflessness. It's not about agreeing on every detail, but about aligning around one purpose — *to exalt Jesus.*

The enemy knows this, which is why he fights unity harder than anything else. He doesn't mind music without power, or worship without love — but he fears oneness, because that's where the glory falls.

When we worship as one — not competing but completing each other — heaven hears a familiar sound. It's the sound of Eden restored, the echo of heaven's harmony.

Paul urged the church in Ephesians 4:3, *"Make every effort to keep the unity of the Spirit through the bond of peace."* It takes effort. Unity doesn't happen by accident; it's a choice made daily — to forgive, to listen, to prefer others, to stay soft before God and one another.

When hearts are united, the Spirit flows freely. Disunity is like a kink in the hose; it stops the flow. But unity opens the channel for the presence of God to move unhindered.

The Power of "One Accord"

When a worship team, a church, or even a family operates in unity, they carry a collective authority that shakes atmospheres.

Jesus said in Matthew 18:19–20, *"If two of you agree on earth about anything they ask, it will be done for them by My Father in heaven. For where two or three gather in My name, there am I with them."*

Agreement invites His presence; unity sustains it.

It's not about how loud we sing or how long we play — it's about how deeply we love.

When worshippers unite in humility and heart, the Spirit of God breathes upon their sound. It becomes more than music — it becomes ministry.

Lessons from the Oil and the Dew

Psalm 133 gives two images of unity — **oil and dew.**
Oil speaks of anointing. It flows downward — from the head (Christ) to the body (the Church). That means unity is sustained when we stay aligned with the Head, Jesus Himself.
Dew speaks of refreshing. It falls quietly, consistently, and brings life wherever it lands. Unity refreshes — it revives weary hearts and restores joy to worship.
Oil empowers; dew renews.
Both descend when brethren dwell together in unity.

Reflection: Are We Making One Sound?

Take a moment and ask yourself:

- ✓ *Am I adding to unity or breaking it?*
- ✓ *Do I celebrate others' gifts as much as my own?*
- ✓ *Do I pray for the people I lead and serve with?*
- ✓ *Can heaven hear one sound from our hearts, or are we playing different tunes?*

Unity is costly — it demands humility. But when we lay down pride and pick up love, we create an environment where the glory of God rests continually. When the worship team becomes one in heart, the congregation catches it — and soon, the entire house becomes one sound before God.

A Worshipper's Prayer

"Father, make us one.
One in heart, one in purpose, one in spirit.

Forgive us for every moment we've allowed ego, offense, or pride to divide us. Teach us to value people over position, and presence over performance.
Let our rehearsals become prayer circles and our songs become love offerings. As the trumpeters and singers were one, let us become one — that Your glory may fill the house again.
May our unity release a sound that draws heaven close and melts hearts before You. We don't just want harmony in music; we want harmony in love. In Jesus' name, Amen."

When worshippers unite, the heavens open. When hearts beat in one rhythm, the Spirit finds rest. For God does not dwell where there is division — He inhabits the harmony of His people.
And when that sound rises — one sound, one heart, one love — heaven bends low to listen.

Brokenness — The Fragrance That Fills the Room

There is a kind of worship that doesn't come from joy, excitement, or celebration. It comes from pain. From surrender. From a heart that's been shattered — yet still chooses to sing.

This is the worship that moves heaven.

It's not the loudest, but it's the most fragrant.

It's not polished, but it's pure.

It's the worship born from brokenness — the fragrance that fills the room when a soul pours itself out before God.

David understood this when he wrote in Psalm 34:18, *"The Lord is close to the brokenhearted and saves those who are crushed in spirit."*

And again, in Psalm 51:17, he confessed,

"The sacrifices of God are a broken spirit; a broken and contrite heart, O God, You will not despise."

He didn't say God delights in a perfect heart — He delights in a broken one. Because when our hearts break, His grace rushes in. Brokenness is not the end of worship; it's the beginning of true worship.

Hannah: Pouring Out Her Soul

In 1 Samuel 1, we find a woman named Hannah, whose story paints a portrait of raw, desperate worship.

Year after year, she went up to the house of the Lord, carrying the silent ache of barrenness. The taunts of Peninnah, her husband's other wife, cut deep. Though Elkanah loved her, his words — *"Am I not better to you than ten sons?"* — could not soothe the void she felt.

One day, Hannah could take no more. The weight of unfulfilled prayers drove her to the altar. There, she *"wept bitterly and prayed to the Lord."* (1 Samuel 1:10)

She wasn't eloquent. She didn't bring a song, a sacrifice, or a public prayer. She brought herself — trembling, tear-stained, and broken.

Eli, the priest, thought she was drunk because her lips moved but no words came out. But the Scripture says, *"She was speaking in her heart."* (v.13)

That's where true worship happens — in the heart.

And then Hannah said something that changed everything:

"I am a woman deeply troubled… I have been pouring out my soul before the Lord." (v.15)

Pouring out — that's what broken worship is. It's not pretending you're fine. It's bringing the real, raw, unedited version of yourself before a holy God and saying, "Here I am."

And what did God do with her brokenness? He turned it into birthing.

From her tears came a prophet — Samuel — who would anoint kings and shape Israel's destiny.

Hannah's worship wasn't pretty, but it was powerful. She didn't sing her way to breakthrough; she wept her way there.

Brokenness became the womb of her miracle.

The Woman with the Alabaster Jar

Centuries later, another woman would teach the same truth — that brokenness releases fragrance.

In Mark 14:3–9, we read about a woman who came to Jesus while He was reclining at a table in Bethany. She carried an alabaster jar of very costly perfume —

worth an entire year's wages. Without hesitation, she broke the jar and poured it on His head.

The disciples were indignant. "Why this waste?" they asked. "This perfume could have been sold and the money given to the poor."

But Jesus silenced them with a profound truth:

"Leave her alone. She has done a beautiful thing to Me." (v.6)

Beautiful — not because it was extravagant, but because it was broken.

She didn't open the jar carefully; she *broke* it. There was no plan to save any for later. Her act was final, complete, irreversible. That's what true worship looks like — a heart so surrendered that it holds nothing back.

When she broke the jar, the room filled with fragrance. And two thousand years later, we still smell it in the pages of Scripture.

Brokenness releases what's inside. As long as the jar remains unbroken, the perfume stays hidden. But when it's shattered, what's precious inside spills out and fills the atmosphere with beauty.

The same is true for us. The fragrance of our lives is released when our pride, control, and self-sufficiency are broken before God.

The woman's broken jar became her song, her surrender, her sermon.

And Jesus said, *"Wherever the gospel is preached throughout the world, what she has done will also be told, in memory of her."* (v.9)

Her broken worship became her legacy.

Broken but Beautiful — The Story of Leah

Leah had been part of the worship team at her church for years. Her voice carried both power and tenderness — but lately, she had lost her spark.

A painful divorce had left her heart shattered. She still came to church, still led songs, still smiled — but inside, she was numb.

One Sunday morning, as she stood on stage, the song began: *"You are good, good, oh…"*

She couldn't sing it. Her throat tightened. Her hands trembled. She turned away from the microphone and wept.

For the first time in months, she didn't perform — she *poured out.*

After the service, she knelt alone by the altar and whispered, "God, I don't even have words left. All I have is this broken heart. But it's Yours."

That day, something changed. It wasn't dramatic or loud. It was quiet — like a gentle healing wind passing through her soul. She later said, "I realized that my brokenness wasn't disqualifying me from worship — it was drawing me closer to it."

Over time, her worship deepened. Her songs carried more weight, more compassion. People often wept when she sang, not because of vocal perfection, but because of spiritual authenticity.

Leah had learned what Hannah and the alabaster woman already knew: the most beautiful worship often rises from the most broken hearts.

The Beauty of a Cracked Vessel

In ancient times, potters sometimes repaired cracked clay pots by filling the cracks with gold or silver — a process known as *kintsugi.* The finished vessel, though broken, became more beautiful than before.

Its fractures told a story — not of weakness, but of redemption.

That's how God works with worshippers. He doesn't discard the broken ones. He mends them with mercy, fills them with grace, and turns their cracks into places where His glory shines through.

David was a broken man when he wrote Psalm 51 — shattered by guilt after his sin with Bathsheba. Yet out of his repentance came one of the most powerful songs of worship in Scripture:

"Create in me a clean heart, O God, and renew a right spirit within me." (v.10)

David didn't try to hide his failure; he turned it into fragrance. His confession became worship. His brokenness became beauty.

That's why broken worship is precious to God — it carries the aroma of humility.

When Pain Becomes Praise

Every worshipper faces seasons of brokenness — loss, betrayal, unanswered prayers, disappointment. Those are the moments the enemy whispers, *"You have nothing left to give."*

But heaven whispers back, *"Give Me your tears."*

The Lord doesn't waste brokenness; He transforms it. Every tear shed in His presence becomes oil poured at His feet.

He collects them, cherishes them, and turns them into fragrance.

In Revelation 5:8, the golden bowls in heaven are said to be *"full of incense, which are the prayers of the saints."* Can you imagine? Your tears, your sighs, your whispered prayers — bottled as perfume before the throne of God.

That's how precious your broken worship is.

God's Nearness in the Broken Place

When everything falls apart, we often assume God has gone silent. But Scripture says the opposite: *"The Lord is near to the brokenhearted."* (Psalm 34:18)

He is not repelled by pain; He is drawn to it.

When the pieces of your heart scatter, His presence gathers them. When your song falters, His Spirit carries it. When your faith feels fragile, His mercy holds it together.

You don't have to hide your wounds from Him. He already sees them — and He calls them beautiful when offered in surrender.

Reflection: What's in My Jar?

Ask yourself:

- ✓ *Am I holding on to something that God is asking me to break?*
- ✓ *Is my worship still guarded and measured, or have I truly poured myself out?*
- ✓ *Do I bring only my strength to God, or do I also bring my scars?*

Brokenness is not a weakness to hide — it's a fragrance to release.

When we pour ourselves out completely before Him, withholding nothing, heaven responds. The fragrance fills the room — and more importantly, it fills His heart.

A Worshipper's Prayer

Father, I come with my broken pieces — my fears, my failures, my pain. I lay them before You as my offering. I don't have perfection to give, but I give You my honesty.

Like Hannah, I pour out my soul. Like the woman with the alabaster jar, I break what's costly to me. Take my brokenness, Lord, and make it beautiful. Let the fragrance of surrender fill the room — and may You be pleased. In Jesus' name, Amen.

Brokenness is not the absence of strength — it is the presence of surrender. And when a heart breaks open before God, heaven leans close, and the fragrance of that moment never fades.
For in the Kingdom, broken vessels release the most beautiful perfume.

The Cost of the Call — Carrying the Weight of Worship

Every true call carries a cost.
Every anointing carries a weight.
Worship is not just a privilege — it is a responsibility.
Those who are called to carry God's presence must also be willing to carry His burden.
There is a price to pay for those who would lead others into the Holy of Holies — the price of purity, humility, perseverance, and often, pain.
The call to worship is beautiful, but it is not light.
Jesus said in Luke 9:23, *"Whoever wants to be My disciple must deny themselves and take up their cross daily and follow Me."*
And in Romans 12:1, Paul writes,
"Therefore, I urge you, brothers and sisters, in view of God's mercy, to offer your bodies as a living sacrifice, holy and pleasing to God — this is your true and proper worship."
True worship is not found in the songs we sing, but in the sacrifices we make.
To lead others before the throne, we must first learn to kneel before it ourselves.

David — The Price of His Presence
Few understood the cost of worship more than David.
In 2 Samuel 24, after David's sin of taking a census brought a plague upon Israel, the prophet Gad instructed him to build an altar to the Lord on the threshing floor of Araunah.
When David approached Araunah to buy the land, the man offered to give it freely — the oxen, the

wood, the sacrifice. It was all ready. But David refused.
He said these unforgettable words:
"No, I will not offer to the Lord my God that which costs me nothing." (2 Samuel 24:24)
David knew worship without cost is hollow. True worship always requires something of us — time, pride, comfort, convenience, or reputation.
That altar became a sacred place, not because of what was sacrificed on it, but because of the heart that gave it.
In David's story, we learn this truth: the greater the call, the higher the cost. And the higher the cost, the deeper the intimacy with God.

Moses — Bearing the Weight of God's Glory
In **Exodus 33**, Moses cried out, *"Show me Your glory."*
It sounds like a beautiful prayer — but God knew what Moses was asking for. Glory isn't light; it's *weight.* The Hebrew word for "glory" (*kabod*) literally means "heaviness."
To carry the glory of God is to carry His weight — His holiness, His burden for people, His passion for purity.
When Moses came down from Mount Sinai, his face shone so brightly that people couldn't even look at him. But that glow came at a price: forty days in God's presence, fasting, isolated, and humbled.
He carried the weight of divine encounter — and with it, the responsibility of leadership, intercession, and sacrifice.
Every worshipper who longs for the glory of God must be ready to bear its weight. The glory is not

ornamental; it's *transformational.* It will test your motives, refine your heart, and expose your flesh.
The glory costs — but it's worth every tear.

Mary — The Cost of Carrying His Presence
No one embodied the cost of divine calling like Mary, the mother of Jesus.
When the angel Gabriel told her she would bear the Son of God, her life instantly changed. Her reputation, her engagement, her comfort — all placed at risk.
Yet her response was simple and surrendered:
"Be it unto me according to Your word." (Luke 1:38)
Mary carried not just a promise but a Person — literally, the Presence of God — within her.
And with that privilege came pain: whispers of scandal, the weight of misunderstanding, the agony of watching her Son suffer.
But Mary's "yes" changed history.
Every worshipper who says "yes" to God carries something sacred inside — and must also bear the cost of that calling.
There will be seasons of waiting, rejection, loneliness, and spiritual warfare. But like Mary, our surrender births glory that outlives us.

Paul — The Weight of Ministry
In the New Testament, the apostle Paul's entire life was an example of carrying the cost of the call.
He wrote in 2 Corinthians 4:7–10,
"We have this treasure in jars of clay to show that this all-surpassing power is from God and not from us. We are hard pressed on every side, but not crushed; perplexed, but not in despair; persecuted, but not abandoned; struck down, but not destroyed."

Paul carried the treasure — the presence of Christ — in a fragile human vessel. And it cost him dearly: persecution, imprisonment, hunger, and betrayal.

But through every hardship, he discovered the secret: that the presence of God inside him was greater than any pressure around him.

Those who carry His presence must also carry His heart — and His heart breaks for the world.

That's the weight of worship — to feel what He feels, to love who He loves, and to stay faithful even when no one applauds.

The Story of Caleb — The Cost of Staying True

Caleb had been serving on the worship team for nearly fifteen years. He'd seen growth, revival, and change — but lately, he'd also seen conflict. A younger generation had risen, bringing new styles, new songs, and new sounds.

Many of his peers stepped away, frustrated that their era seemed forgotten. But Caleb stayed — not because it was easy, but because he had made a covenant with God, not a contract with a ministry.

There were times he felt invisible, unappreciated, even misunderstood. Yet he kept showing up early, praying over every rehearsal, helping younger musicians tune their instruments, and mentoring them in humility.

One evening, a young singer named Leah pulled him aside and said, *"Caleb, thank you for staying. Your quiet faithfulness has taught me more than any workshop."*

Tears filled his eyes. At that moment, he realized something profound: *the cost of the call is not always paid in public suffering, but in private faithfulness.*

Caleb learned that carrying the weight of worship is not glamorous — it's often hidden, heavy, and holy. But heaven sees every sacrifice.

The Weight and the Reward

There's a paradox to this calling — the same presence that breaks us also builds us. The same glory that humbles us also heals us.

Carrying the weight of worship may mean:

- ✓ Forgiving when it's hard.
- ✓ Serving when it's unseen.
- ✓ Staying pure when it's unpopular.
- ✓ Obeying when it costs reputation or comfort.
- ✓ But every cost is an investment in eternity.

Jesus Himself paid the ultimate price. Philippians 2:8 says,

"He humbled Himself by becoming obedient to death — even death on a cross."

He was the perfect worshipper — and His obedience changed the world.

If the One we worship paid such a price, how can we expect to follow Him without carrying a cross of our own?

Reflection: Am I Willing to Pay the Price?

Ask yourself:

- ✓ *Do I still say "yes" to God when it costs me something?*
- ✓ *Am I serving for convenience, or out of covenant?*
- ✓ *Am I willing to carry the weight of His glory, not just the sound of His songs?*

Worship is not cheap. The anointing is costly oil — and every drop is pressed out through surrender.

When you carry the weight of worship, you become part of something eternal. And though the price is high, the presence is worth it.

A Worshipper's Prayer

Father, thank You for calling me to carry Your presence. I know this call is holy and heavy — teach me to bear it well. When I'm tempted to quit, remind me of the privilege of serving You. When it costs me comfort, help me see the glory beyond the pain. Make me faithful in the hidden things and steadfast in the hard things. Like David, may I never offer You what costs me nothing. Like Mary, may I always say, "Be it unto me." And like Jesus, may I carry my cross with joy, knowing resurrection follows. In Your name, Amen.

The Weight of Glory

C.S. Lewis once wrote that "the weight of glory" is both beautiful and unbearable — a reminder that God entrusts His presence not to the gifted, but to the surrendered.

When you carry His presence rightly, it transforms not just your music but your life. It purifies your motives, refines your heart, and deepens your dependence.

Yes, there is a cost to the call.

But those who pay it discover what David, Moses, Mary, and Paul all knew — that the presence of God is worth any price.

For when you've tasted His glory, no sacrifice feels too great.

True Worship Always Leads to Transformation

True worship is never a one-way act.
When we truly encounter God, we are never the same.
Worship, at its core, is not just about giving to God — it's also about *becoming* like Him. The more we behold Him, the more His image begins to shape us.
True worship doesn't just move heaven — it moves *us*.
The apostle Paul wrote in 2 Corinthians 3:18,
"And we all, who with unveiled faces contemplate the Lord's glory, are being transformed into His image with ever-increasing glory, which comes from the Lord, who is the Spirit."
Notice the connection — *beholding leads to becoming.*
When we fix our gaze on the glory of the Lord, transformation happens naturally. You cannot truly see Him and remain unchanged. Every authentic encounter with His presence shifts something within you — your priorities, your desires, your attitudes, even your countenance.
Paul echoes this again in Romans 12:2,
"Do not be conformed to this world, but be transformed by the renewing of your mind. Then you will be able to test and approve what God's will is — His good, pleasing and perfect will."
Transformation begins not with effort, but with exposure — being exposed to His presence, His truth, and His love until what is unlike Him begins to fade.

If our worship doesn't change us, it hasn't really reached Him.

Isaiah: From Woe to Worship to Witness

In Isaiah 6, we find one of the most powerful examples of transformation through worship.

Isaiah had been serving as a prophet — faithful, articulate, perhaps even respected among his peers. But then something happened that changed everything.

"In the year that King Uzziah died, I saw the Lord, high and exalted, seated on a throne; and the train of His robe filled the temple." (Isaiah 6:1)

Isaiah didn't just hear about God — he *saw* Him. And in that vision, everything shifted.

The seraphim cried, *"Holy, holy, holy is the Lord Almighty; the whole earth is full of His glory."* (v.3)

And Isaiah's immediate response wasn't joy or excitement. It was *conviction.* He cried, *"Woe to me! I am ruined! For I am a man of unclean lips, and I live among a people of unclean lips."* (v.5)

When you truly encounter God's holiness, you see your own humanity. Worship doesn't flatter you; it reveals you.

But God didn't leave Isaiah in condemnation. One of the seraphim took a live coal from the altar and touched his lips, saying, *"Your guilt is taken away and your sin atoned for."* (v.7)

That moment — that act of cleansing — transformed Isaiah from a fearful man to a faithful messenger.

Then came the divine question:

- ✓ *"Whom shall I send, and who will go for Us?"*
- ✓ *Isaiah didn't hesitate. "Here am I. Send me."*

That's the mark of true worship — it ends not just with a song, but with a surrender. Worshippers who truly see God are always ready to say yes to His call. Isaiah entered the temple a prophet — he left a messenger. He came burdened — he left burning. Worship changed him.

Saul to Paul: Worship Through Encounter

The New Testament gives us another dramatic example of transformation — Saul of Tarsus.

Before his encounter with Christ, Saul was zealous, religious, and ruthless. He believed he was serving God by persecuting Christians. He had the law, the intellect, and the passion — but he didn't have relationship.

Then one day, on the road to Damascus, heaven interrupted his journey.

"As he neared Damascus on his journey, suddenly a light from heaven flashed around him. He fell to the ground and heard a voice say, 'Saul, Saul, why do you persecute Me?'" (Acts 9:3–4)

Saul was stunned. He responded, *"Who are You, Lord?"*

And the answer came, *"I am Jesus, whom you are persecuting."*

In that moment, Saul's theology crumbled, and his heart was undone. He was struck blind — a symbol of the darkness that had consumed his understanding — and led helplessly into the city.

Three days later, a disciple named Ananias came, laid hands on him, and said,

"Brother Saul, the Lord Jesus, who appeared to you on the road as you were coming here, has sent me so that you may see again and be filled with the Holy Spirit." (v.17)

Scales fell from Saul's eyes, and he could see again — not just physically, but spiritually.

That encounter with Jesus transformed a persecutor into an apostle, a destroyer into a disciple, a man of wrath into a messenger of grace.

Every time Saul worshipped thereafter, it wasn't ritual — it was remembrance. He knew firsthand the God who redeems and restores. That's why he could write later, "I have been crucified with Christ, and it is no longer I who live, but Christ who lives in me." (Galatians 2:20)

The man who once sang the praises of religion now sang the praises of redemption.

Worship changed Saul's direction, his heart, his identity, and even his name.

From Stage to Secret Change — The Story of Marcus

Marcus had been leading worship for years. He was known for his stage presence, his powerful vocals, and his ability to move a crowd. People often said, "When Marcus sings, you can feel heaven."

But privately, Marcus knew something was missing.

He was good at *leading others into God's presence* — but rarely stayed there himself. Worship had become familiar, almost professional. His songs stirred others, but they no longer stirred him.

One night after rehearsal, Marcus stayed behind. The church was dark and empty, the lights dimmed, and only the faint hum of the speakers filled the air. He sat at the piano and whispered, "Lord, why do I feel so empty?"

And in that stillness, he sensed the Holy Spirit whisper, *"You've been performing for Me, but you haven't been with Me."*

Those words pierced him. Tears filled his eyes. He began to play softly and pray — really pray. No microphone, no audience, just him and God. He confessed his pride, his distance, his weariness.

Something broke inside him that night — but not in a painful way. It was like a wall collapsing. And in its place came peace.

Over the weeks that followed, Marcus began to notice subtle changes. His patience deepened. His love for people grew. His worship became less about perfection and more about presence. He found himself weeping more — not from sadness, but from gratitude.

One Sunday, after leading a simple song, he looked out at the congregation and said, "Friends, I used to think worship changed atmospheres. But I've learned — true worship changes *hearts*."

Marcus had discovered the truth: transformation is the fruit of authentic worship.

Beholding to Becoming

Worship is not just about singing to God — it's about *seeing* God. And when we see Him clearly, we start reflecting Him naturally.

Just as Moses' face shone after being in God's presence (Exodus 34:29), our lives begin to glow with His nature when we spend time before Him. You can always tell who has been with Jesus — their words carry grace, their hearts radiate kindness, and their eyes carry peace.

Transformation is the true test of worship. If your encounters with God don't make you more loving, more humble, more forgiving, then it's time to ask, "Have I truly beheld Him, or have I just sung about Him?"

The goal of worship is not emotional high — it's inner change.

Every genuine worship experience should bring us closer to Christ's likeness — one degree at a time, one song at a time, one surrender at a time.

From Glory to Glory

Transformation is rarely instantaneous. It's often gradual — *"from glory to glory."* Each encounter leaves us slightly more like Him, until one day, we look back and realize we've been shaped by His hand all along.

Sometimes, transformation looks like conviction. Other times, it looks like healing. Sometimes it's a changed habit; other times, it's a softened heart.

But always, it's a reflection of His nature being formed in ours.

True worship doesn't end when the music stops. It continues in how we love, how we serve, how we forgive, how we live.

The measure of our worship is not how high our hands go, but how low our hearts bow.

Daily Surrender: The Transformation Checklist

Here's a simple question to carry each day:

"Am I being transformed or just performing?"

Ask yourself:

- ✓ *Do I leave worship more humble than I entered?*
- ✓ *Is my character being refined as much as my craft?*
- ✓ *Do I love people better after being in His presence?*
- ✓ *Have my thoughts, words, or habits shifted toward holiness?*

Transformation is not proven by applause — it's proven by fruit.
As Jesus said, *"You will know them by their fruits."* (Matthew 7:16)
The truest worshippers are those who resemble the One they worship.

Reflection: Becoming the Song

When a worshipper is transformed, their life becomes the song. They don't just *sing* about grace — they *live* it. They don't just *declare* holiness — they *demonstrate* it.
Isaiah was changed by one vision. Saul was changed by one encounter. Marcus was changed by one honest moment.
All three discovered that the closer you draw to God, the less you can stay the same.
Because worship isn't about music changing the mood — it's about God changing the man.

A Worshipper's Prayer

Father, I don't want to just sing — I want to change. Let my worship shape me into the likeness of Your Son. Expose anything in me that doesn't look like You.
Renew my mind, cleanse my heart, and transform my desires. Like Isaiah, touch my lips with Your fire. Like Paul, open my eyes to see You clearly. Like Marcus, teach me to dwell, not just perform. Let every encounter with You make me more like You — until my life becomes the song You love to hear. In Jesus' name, Amen.

Transformation is the ultimate goal of true worship. It's not about leaving church impressed; it's about leaving changed. When worship touches heaven, heaven touches the worshipper — and that touch leaves an imprint that no song, stage, or sermon could ever achieve.

For every true worshipper carries this testimony: "I went into His presence one way... and came out another."

Character Before Chords — Guarding the Legacy

Every generation inherits a song — but not every generation inherits the heart behind it.
The true test of a worshipper's life is not how many songs they've sung, how many albums they've released, or how many platforms they've stood upon. The true test is what remains when their voice grows quiet — *what kind of worshippers follow after them.*
Worship has always been God's generational language. Each generation receives a melody from heaven and is called to pass it on. But God never intended for us to pass on mere music — He calls us to pass on *character.*
That's why Scripture reminds us in Psalm 145:4,
"One generation shall praise Your works to another, and shall declare Your mighty acts."
It's not just a call to keep singing — it's a call to keep *living faithfully.*
Paul captured the same heart when he wrote to Timothy, *"And the things you have heard from me in the presence of many witnesses, entrust to reliable men who will also be qualified to teach others."* (2 Timothy 2:2)
Four generations are hidden in that verse — Paul → Timothy → faithful men → others. That's legacy.
Legacy is not about leaving a name behind; it's about leaving a nature behind.

David and the Sons of Asaph — Training for More Than Talent
Few understood this better than King David.

David was not only Israel's greatest warrior and king — he was its greatest worshipper. Yet, toward the end of his life, we find him doing something deeply significant: *training the next generation of worshippers.*
1 Chronicles 25:1–6 paints the picture:
"David, together with the commanders of the army, set apart some of the sons of Asaph, Heman, and Jeduthun for the ministry of prophesying, accompanied by harps, lyres, and cymbals… All these men were under the supervision of their fathers for the music in the temple of the Lord."
David didn't just appoint skilled musicians — he *trained* worshippers. He taught them not only how to play but how to prophesy. Not just how to perform, but how to minister.
Notice that phrase — *"under the supervision of their fathers."*
David understood something powerful: worship is a family calling. It's passed on, father to son, mentor to disciple, generation to generation.
He didn't gather the most famous singers; he gathered the most faithful hearts. He knew that the presence of God could not be sustained by talent alone — it required trust, purity, and humility.
David invested in Asaph, Heman, and Jeduthun — and they, in turn, trained their sons. The result? Generations of Levites who continued the worship ministry long after David was gone.
Even centuries later, during Nehemiah's time, when the temple was rebuilt, the *sons of Asaph* were still there — singing, serving, and worshipping (Nehemiah 11:22).
That's legacy.

David's songs faded with time, but his spirit of worship lived on through those he discipled.
He didn't just pass down melodies — he passed down *motives*. He didn't just leave behind songs — he left behind *servants of the Lord*.

Paul and Timothy—Legacy Through Relationship
In the New Testament, Paul models the same pattern with Timothy.
Paul didn't treat Timothy like an assistant; he treated him like a son. He wrote,
"To Timothy, my true son in the faith." (1 Timothy 1:2)
Paul knew that legacy is built through relationship, not instruction alone.
He didn't simply tell Timothy what to preach — he showed him how to live. He spoke of enduring hardship, keeping the faith, and guarding integrity.
In 2 Timothy 3:10–11, Paul says,
"You, however, know all about my teaching, my way of life, my purpose, faith, patience, love, endurance, persecutions, and sufferings."
Do you see the order?
Teaching came first — but *way of life* followed immediately.
Paul wasn't content with passing on doctrine; he passed on *example*.
Timothy became a reflection of Paul's faithfulness because he walked closely enough to catch his heart. And in time, Timothy too would entrust the same truth to others.
That's how the flame keeps burning — not through performances, but through people.

Ethan — The Worship Mentor

Ethan had served as a worship leader for over thirty years. He had seen trends come and go — from choirs to bands, from hymnals to digital sets, from reverence to raw emotion. Through it all, he had one conviction: *the presence of God must remain central.*

Now in his sixties, his voice wasn't what it used to be. Younger worship leaders were taking the stage, and the spotlight was shifting. But instead of feeling replaced, Ethan felt *released.*

He began mentoring a small group of young musicians — Daniel, Grace, and Michael — all eager, gifted, and hungry for the anointing.

At first, they expected Ethan to teach them chord progressions, song arrangements, and worship set structures. But what they received went far deeper.

He taught them about heart posture before soundcheck, about praying for the congregation before singing to them, about walking in forgiveness when hurt, and about guarding purity when praised.

One evening, after rehearsal, Ethan gathered them around and said quietly, "Someday, people will forget the songs I've sung. But if I've taught you how to *walk humbly before God*, then I've succeeded."

Those words stayed with them.

Years later, after Ethan's passing, Daniel wrote a song called *"Legacy of the Heart."* It began with these words: *"He taught me how to worship loud, But live quietly before the King. He showed me that the truest sound Is a heart that's clean when it sings."*

That song spread far beyond their church. Not because of clever lyrics — but because it carried Ethan's spirit.

That's legacy. You reproduce who you are — not what you sing.

The Power of Character in the Line of Worship

In every generation, God looks for worshippers who will not just carry a song but carry a *standard.*

Skill impresses; character imparts.

Talent may attract crowds, but integrity attracts the glory of God.

When worshippers live rightly, they release an aroma that outlasts their voice. Long after the stage lights fade, their influence continues through the lives they've touched and the hearts they've shaped.

That's why building a legacy is not about raising performers — it's about raising *priests.* People who know how to minister before the Lord with clean hands and pure hearts.

Guarding the Legacy

A legacy doesn't protect itself — it must be guarded.

That means every worship leader, every musician, every mentor must be intentional about modeling humility, accountability, and holiness.

Just as David prepared the next generation, we must train ours — not in performance but in purity, not in chords but in character.

We must teach them:

- ✓ That private prayer is more important than public applause.
- ✓ That obedience is more lasting than opportunity.
- ✓ That holiness is more powerful than hype.

The songs we teach may fade, but the spirit we impart will echo through eternity.

When the next generation sees us live with integrity, they will follow not just our sound but our steps.

When Legacy Outlives the Stage

Years after Ethan's death, his old leather Bible still sat on the music stand in the church rehearsal room. The cover was worn, the pages filled with notes, prayers, and tears.

Every new worship leader who joined the team was told the same thing: *"That Bible belonged to a man who never chased fame — only God."*

Before each rehearsal, someone would open it and read a few of his handwritten words:

"Worship is not what you do — it's who you are when no one's looking."

The presence in that room was different. It was as if his devotion still lingered — like incense that never stopped burning.

That's the beauty of a guarded legacy: when a life of worship outlives the worshipper.

Reflection: What Am I Passing On?

Someday, your voice will fade, your hands will grow weak, your position may change — but your influence will continue through those who watched you worship.

Ask yourself:

- ✓ *What will my worship leave behind?*
- ✓ *Am I raising performers or disciples?*
- ✓ *Will the next generation know more about my songs — or my Savior?*

Every choice you make today writes the legacy of tomorrow.

You can either leave behind echoes of sound or imprints of spirit.

Choose the latter.

A Worshipper's Prayer

Father, help me build what lasts. Teach me to value character more than chords, integrity more than influence, and faithfulness more than fame. Like David, let me raise others who know You deeply. Like Paul, let me entrust truth to faithful hearts. May those who come after me not just inherit my songs, but my surrender. Let my legacy be love, my testimony be truth, and my song be remembered not for its melody, but for its purity. In Jesus' name, Amen.

True legacy is not found in music charts or ministry titles. It's found in lives transformed because you walked faithfully before God.

When your chords have stopped and your name fades from the program, may generations still rise and say — *"He didn't just lead us in worship. He showed us how to live it."*

That's character before chords. That's a legacy worth guarding.

The Overflow — Worship That Touches the World

True worship never ends where it begins. It starts in the secret place, flows into the sanctuary, and then spills out into the streets.

When worship is real, it cannot be contained within a church wall or confined to a melody — it *overflows.* It changes atmospheres, influences culture, heals hearts, and reveals Christ.

Worship that touches heaven will inevitably touch earth. Because when a heart is full of God, it will naturally spill Him everywhere it goes.

The River that Flows from the Temple

In Ezekiel 47, the prophet saw a vision of a river flowing from the temple of God.

It began as a trickle from beneath the threshold — small, almost unnoticed. But as it flowed, it grew deeper. First ankle-deep, then knee-deep, then waist-deep — until it became a river no one could cross.

"Wherever the river flows, everything will live." (Ezekiel 47:9)

That river represents the life and presence of God flowing out of His dwelling place — and today, *we* are that temple (1 Corinthians 6:19).

When we worship, something begins to flow. The presence that fills us begins to move through us, carrying healing, hope, and holiness into dry places.

The purpose of worship was never just to fill us; it was to make us *fountains.*

The truest measure of worship is not how full we feel — but how much life flows out of us afterward.

The Early Church — Worship that Turned the World Upside Down

After Pentecost, the early believers didn't simply stay in the upper room enjoying the presence of God — they carried it into every corner of their world.

Acts 2:46–47 says,

"Every day they continued to meet together in the temple courts. They broke bread in their homes and ate together with glad and sincere hearts, praising God and enjoying the favor of all the people. And the Lord added to their number daily those who were being saved."

Notice the rhythm — worship and witness intertwined.

They worshipped *together* and then *lived* their worship out loud. Their praise didn't end with music; it continued through meals, generosity, and compassion.

The result? The Lord added daily.

Their worship was attractive not because of their excellence, but because of their authenticity. The same Spirit that fell in the upper room overflowed into the marketplace, the neighborhoods, and even prisons (Acts 16:25).

Paul and Silas sang in chains, and their song set others free.

That's what happens when worship overflows — it breaks chains beyond our own.

Mary of Bethany — Worship that Becomes Witness

When Mary broke her alabaster jar and poured it over Jesus, she wasn't trying to make a statement — but she did.

Her private act of devotion became a public testimony. Jesus said,

"Wherever the gospel is preached throughout the world, what she has done will also be told, in memory of her." (Mark 14:9)

Her fragrance filled not only that room but generations to come.

That's the power of worship that overflows — it lingers. It becomes witness. It leaves a trail of God's presence wherever it goes.

David — Worship that Influenced a Nation

In the Old Testament, David's personal worship didn't just transform his life — it transformed a nation. His songs became Israel's prayers. His psalms became their hymnal. His private passion for God became a public culture of praise.

When he brought the Ark of the Covenant to Jerusalem (2 Samuel 6), he danced before the Lord with all his might — not as a king, but as a worshipper. His authenticity stirred the people to do the same.

David's personal overflow became national revival.

That's what real worship does — it spreads. It ignites hearts around it.

Olivia — Worship Beyond the Walls

Olivia wasn't a singer, musician, or leader. She was a schoolteacher — gentle, faithful, and quietly passionate about Jesus.

Every morning before her class arrived, she would sit at her desk, whispering a simple prayer: "Lord, let my classroom be filled with Your peace."

Over the years, something remarkable happened. Students who walked in anxious would often leave calmer. Parents remarked how their children felt "safe" in her class. Even fellow teachers noticed that Olivia carried an unusual calmness.

One day, a colleague asked, "What's your secret? You never seem flustered." Olivia smiled softly and said, "I worship before I work."

Her worship was not a song — it was her *spirit.*

She didn't need a stage to lead worship; her life *was* a stage. Her kindness, patience, and quiet faith became the melody others heard.

At her retirement ceremony, one student — now grown — said through tears, "You taught us more about God through the way you lived than through any lesson."

Olivia's life was proof that when worship truly fills the heart, it overflows into every place our feet tread.

When Worship Becomes Mission

The ultimate purpose of worship is not just personal renewal but divine representation. When we worship, we are being filled — but when we leave worship, we are being *sent.*

Jesus told the Samaritan woman,

"The Father is seeking those who will worship Him in spirit and in truth." (John 4:23)

But just a few verses later, that same woman — who had come for water — ran back to her town declaring, *"Come, see a Man who told me everything I ever did!"* (John 4:29). One encounter. One moment of worship. And she became an evangelist.

Worshippers make the best witnesses because they don't speak from theory — they speak from encounter. They've *seen* Him, *known* Him, and cannot help but tell others.

The Samaritan woman didn't attend a worship service — she *became* one.
That's the overflow.

Overflow in the Ordinary

Not every overflow looks dramatic. Sometimes it's a word of encouragement at work, a prayer whispered in a hospital hallway, or a smile that carries God's kindness.
When your life is saturated with His presence, even your silence carries His fragrance.
Paul said in 2 Corinthians 2:15,
"For we are to God the pleasing aroma of Christ among those who are being saved and those who are perishing."
You carry His scent wherever you go.

The Fragrance of a Life Well-Lived

The world doesn't need more polished performances; it needs living altars — men and women whose hearts still burn after the song is over.
When worship is genuine, it flows into love for people, justice for the hurting, compassion for the poor, forgiveness toward the undeserving, and mercy toward the broken.
In other words, true worship doesn't stop with hands lifted up — it continues with hands stretched out.
The overflow of worship is seen not in how well we sing, but in how well we serve.

Reflection: Am I Overflowing or Contained?

Ask yourself:

- ✓ *Does my worship reach beyond Sunday?*
- ✓ *Do people encounter Jesus when they encounter me?*

- ✓ *Is the presence I experience in church visible in my attitude, speech, and love outside of it?*

If worship fills us but doesn't flow through us, we've missed its purpose.
Worship is meant to move — from heart to heaven, from heaven to earth, and from us to others.

A Worshipper's Prayer

Father, let my worship overflow. Let what fills me in private spill out in public. Teach me to carry Your presence into every place — my home, my work, my city, my world. Like the river in Ezekiel, let Your Spirit flow through me, bringing life wherever I go. May my words heal, my actions reflect Your kindness, and my heart reveal Your nature. Let my worship become my witness, and my life become Your song to the world. In Jesus' name, Amen.

The Final Note

When worship stays inside the church, it dies in the echo of our songs. But when it overflows into the world, it becomes a movement — a river of life that cannot be stopped.
That's the legacy of every true worshipper: not fame, not performance, not applause — but transformation.
Because at the heart of it all, worship was never meant to end with music. It was meant to begin with it — and continue with *you.*
So go. Carry His presence. Let your worship overflow.
For the sound heaven loves most is not the echo of our chords — but the melody of a life that touches the world.

Conclusion: Worship That Touches Heaven and Changes Earth

Heaven has a sound. It is not the clashing of cymbals, nor the strumming of strings, nor the harmony of choirs—it is the unending cry of hearts completely surrendered to the Lamb.

John saw it in his vision on Patmos. In Revelation 4:8–11, he wrote:

"Day and night they never stop saying: 'Holy, holy, holy is the Lord God Almighty, who was, and is, and is to come.' Whenever the living creatures give glory, honor, and thanks to Him who sits on the throne and who lives for ever and ever, the twenty-four elders fall down before Him who sits on the throne and worship Him who lives for ever and ever. They lay their crowns before the throne and say: 'You are worthy, our Lord and God, to receive glory and honor and power,
for You created all things, and by Your will they were created and have their being.'"

That scene is not a performance—it is a revelation. Every being around the throne is lost in one focus, one Person, one reality: Christ, the Worthy One.

Worship in heaven is not about what can be gained, but what must be given—honor, glory, and surrender. It is the unending echo of hearts overwhelmed by the worthiness of God.

And that, dear worshipper, is what we are invited into.

Our worship on earth is not preparation for eternity
it is participation in it.

Heaven's Pattern, Earth's Mandate

Every time we worship, heaven's atmosphere invades earth's reality. That's what Jesus taught us to pray:

"Your kingdom come, Your will be done, on earth as it is in heaven." (Matthew 6:10)

Worship is heaven's order brought to earth's chaos. It realigns our hearts, our homes, and even our communities to divine rhythm.

But here's the truth few speak about—worship that truly touches heaven will always change the earth. It cannot leave things as they were. It heals, restores, convicts, and rebuilds. Because when God is exalted, everything else finds its rightful place.

When a worshipper kneels, heaven stands ready to move.

From the Altar to the World

In the Old Testament, the fire on the altar of the tabernacle was never to go out. God commanded in Leviticus 6:12–13:

"The fire on the altar must be kept burning; it must not go out."

That same command echoes through every generation of worshippers. The fire that burns privately must never die out publicly.

Worship begins in the heart, but it was always meant to spill over—into families, workplaces, and nations. The altar we build in our secret place becomes the spark that lights the world around us.

Isaiah experienced this in chapter 6: when he saw the Lord high and lifted up, his first response was repentance, but his second was mission. "Here am I, send me." (Isaiah 6:8) Encounter led to

assignment. Worship produced transformation—and transformation birthed purpose.
If our worship only fills the sanctuary but never fuels our obedience, it is incomplete. Worship that touches heaven must also touch earth.

The Worshipper Named Ruth
Ruth was a young woman in her mid-twenties who led worship at a small church in the countryside. She wasn't famous. Her church didn't have bright lights or professional sound. But what they did have was a young woman who carried heaven in her heart.
Each Saturday night, Ruth would sit at her old piano, praying over every song. *"Lord,"* she'd whisper, *"let this draw someone closer to You."* Unknown to her, her quiet faithfulness was touching lives beyond her awareness.
One Sunday, a man named Daniel—recently widowed and bitter at God—wandered into church just to *"sit in the back."* When Ruth began to sing, *"You are faithful, even when I am not,"* something broke in him. He wept uncontrollably. After the service, he told her, *"I came here angry, but your song reminded me that God hadn't left me."*
Ruth smiled through tears and said, "That wasn't my song, Daniel. It was His."
That day, Daniel gave his heart to Jesus. And Ruth realized again that when worship rises from a pure heart, heaven moves, and lives change.
You don't need fame to touch the world—you just need fire.

The Eternal Sound

Someday, every song we've written will fade. Every stage will be dismantled, every instrument silenced. But the worship that comes from the heart—the surrendered life, the daily obedience, the whispered prayers of love—will never cease.

Because worship is not music; it's relationship. It is the continual echo of redeemed hearts saying, *"You are worthy, O Lord."*

Even now, heaven is filled with that sound. And the call to every worshipper is to join that chorus—not for applause, not for recognition, but for love.

The angels will never know what it is to sing from a place of redemption.

Only we can sing, "Worthy is the Lamb who was slain" (Revelation 5:12) — because only we know what it cost Him.

That is the song that touches heaven and changes earth.

Before You Hold a Mic, Hold Your Heart

Before you hold a mic, hold your heart before Him.

Before you step on a platform, step into His presence.

Before you lift your hands before people, lift your soul before your King.

The world measures success by visibility; heaven measures it by surrender.

The stage is fleeting—but the secret place is eternal.

The applause of men fades—but the approval of God resounds forever.

Your highest calling is not to lead worship but to *be* worship.

To live as a temple, a vessel, a heart continually tuned to the frequency of heaven.

Because when your heart belongs to Him fully, everything else—music, ministry, influence—will flow rightly from that center.

The Worshipper's Prayer of Consecration

Father, *I come before You with a grateful and trembling heart. Thank You for the privilege of knowing and worshipping You. Today, I lay down my microphone, my titles, my talents, and even my dreams. I place them at Your feet. Teach me to worship You not just with songs, but with my life. Purify my motives. Align my desires with Yours. Let my private devotion always outweigh my public expression.*

When applause fades, may I still be found worshipping. When crowds are gone, may I still be found kneeling. When trials come, may my worship grow deeper, not quieter.

Make me a carrier of Your presence in every place—my home, my church, my workplace, my world. Let my life become an altar that burns for You alone. Let the fragrance of my worship rise to heaven and the fire of Your glory touch the earth through me.

I surrender afresh. Take all of me, Lord. For You are worthy— now and forever.

In Jesus' name, Amen.

Epilogue: The Final Benediction

The call to worship is not an invitation to performance, but to presence. It is a journey that begins in the heart, continues through the fire, and ends before the throne.

If you remember nothing else from these pages, remember this:

Worship begins where self ends.

May you never lose your wonder, never outgrow your awe, and never stop saying, *"Holy, Holy, Holy." And may your worship—like incense—rise to heaven and fall back as rain upon the earth, watering every life you touch.*

"For from Him and through Him and for Him are all things.

To Him be the glory forever! Amen." — Romans 11:36

About the Author
'GERARD ASSEY'

Gerard Assey is a Graduate in Economics, a PGD in Management (HRD) and holds a Doctorate in Leadership. Gerard holds several International Qualifications in Sales, Debt Collection, Training & Teaching, and is a 'Fellow' of the prestigious 'Institute of Sales & Marketing Management'-UK, a Certified NLP Practitioner, a 'Certified Trainer', an 'Accredited Management Teacher-Behavioral Sciences', a 'Certified Competency Facilitator', a 'Certified Management Consultant'- (the International credentials of a professional management consultant, awarded in accordance with global standards of the ICMCI); and a Certification from the University of Michigan in 'Successful Negotiation: Essential Strategies and Skills'

He is also a Member of the 'National Association of Sales Professionals' backed with several years experience in varied industries, both in India and Overseas. He also holds an 'Etiquette Consultant' Certification from the USA (by Sue Fox, Author of Best Seller: 'Business Etiquette for Dummies'. She has trained some of the top celebrities' world over). He was also a recipient of a scholarship for extensive training in Japan on 'Corporate Management for India'.

Gerard Assey is 'Founder & Chief Corporate Trainer' of the Group: **'Citius, Altius, Fortius Unlimited'**- an organization that **celebrated 20 years of Glorious Service** in 2021, focusing on 3 Core Competencies:

People. Performance. Profit; in functional areas of Sales & Marketing, HR & Organizational Development, covering Recruitment, Training & Consultancy!

Having managed organizations with large Sales Forces in India & Overseas, his specialization cover extensive areas of Sales Training (All levels - Presentation, Negotiation, Key/ Strategic Accounts Management & Managerial Skills for all sectors), Bid Proposal/ Capture Planning/ Management Trainings, Retail Sales, Customer Service & Customer Retention Programs, Training for Prevention & Collection of Debt, Self & Personal Development Programs (Time Management, Teamwork & Team Building, Business Etiquette & Personal Grooming, Leadership & Managerial Skills, People Management Skills, Train-the-Trainer etc), including preparation of Custom-designed Business Manuals for Internal (HR, Induction, and Sales etc) & External use (Instruction, User Manuals).

Gerard has successfully conducted over 6490 Trainings & Workshops (as of Nov '25) all across India, Middle East, Africa, Europe & S.E. Asia. Besides public programs conducted regularly, both in India & Overseas, he has some of the top names as clients whom he services from Single Owners to large Public & Government undertakings, covering all sectors, for their in-house needs.

His website: www.CollectionSkills.com is the only one in this part of the world to be featured in the 'Collections & Credit Risk Magazine-USA' under 'Who's Who in Training' and ranks TOP, along with other websites listed below on most search engines.

Gerard is author of 208 Books already (Nov 2025), all the books being available on all online platforms and outlets as E-books and Paperbacks

A few of our business related books:

1. Bite-sized Bits on Commonsense Management
2. Heart to Heart on Life's Principles'
3. How to become a Successful Manager
4. The Sales Professionals' Master Workbook of S.Y.S.T.E.M.S
5. The Professional Business Email Etiquette Handbook & Guide
6. The Professional Business Video-Conferencing Etiquette Handbook & Guide
7. Professional Presentation Skills
8. Exceptional Customer Service
9. Professional Tele-Marketing Skills
10. Professional Debt Collection Skills
11. The G.R.E.A.T. Sales & Service Workbook
12. Sales Training Advantage for Results (*The Ultimate Sales Training Manual to enable you stand out as a S.T.A.R.*)
13. CEO Daily Planner & Organizer
14. The Sales Professionals' Master Daily Planner
15. The Professional Debt Collector's Master Daily Planner
16. My Daily Planner & Organizer
17. MY EMERGENCY INFORMATION RECORD (Family Emergency & Peace of Mind Planner)
18. The Ultimate Therapist & Counselors Planner and Organizer
19. Building an Ethical Workplace
20. Managing Relationships at Work
21. Managing Business Meetings Effectively
22. Effective Delegation Skills
23. Goal Setting for Success
24. B2B Selling by Email
25. Professional Business Etiquette & Grooming
26. Dining Etiquette & Table Manners
27. Effective Networking Skills
28. Grooming, Etiquette & Manners for Teens, Young Adults & Future Leaders
29. Inter-Personal Skills
30. Get Ready, Get Hired!
31. Selling in a Recession
32. Effective Receivables Management in an Economic Downturn!
33. Real Estate & Property Sales Training
34. Credit Sales & Accounts Receivable Management

35. Selling Skills for Real Estate & Property Advisors
36. Take G.R.E.A.T. C.A.R.E!
37. Spa, Salon & Health Club Selling Skills
38. Selling Travel, Holiday & MICE Services
39. Selling Skills for Spa's, Salons & Health Clubs
40. Retailing in Salons & Spas
41. Selling Holiday, Vacation, Tours & Packages
42. The Power of Sales Referrals
43. Selling Luxury
44. Technical Selling Skills
45. Financial Advisors Sales Training
46. Dealing with Burnout at Work Monopolize Your Markets
47. Selling to Affluent Customers
48. Growing up with Grace
49. Financial Selling Skills
50. *The Effective Manager's Guide: Key Skills to Thrive*
51. From Aspiring to Inspiring: A Guide for New Managers on the Rise
52. The Power of Focus
53. Selling with Integrity: Sell Like Jesus The Perfect Role Model!
54. 31 Habits of Champions: Your 31-Day Journey to Greatness
55. Rejecting Grasshopper Talk: From Grasshopper to Giant-Killer-*Defeating Giants Daily!*
56. Navigate the AI-Powered Future of Bid & Proposals: Up-Skill to Stay Relevant with Alternative Career Paths & Opportunities
57. Hiring Sales Winners
58. Present with Impact
59. Success Unlocked: *Breaking Free from Habits that Hold You Back*
60. Complaints to Cheers, Feedback to Gold: Mastering Complaints Management
61. Thriving Together: *Cultivating Diversity, Equity, and Inclusion*
62. Coaching Skills for Sales Managers
63. Soaring to Success in Business & Leadership: Swifter, Higher, Stronger!
64. From Classroom to Podium: A Student's Guide to Powerful Public Speaking & Presentation Skills
65. Developing Self-Discipline
66. The CEO's 31-Day Power Plan: Unlocking Success through Essential Traits

67. Credibility Matters
68. A Winning Attitude
69. Bid & Proposal Management Using AI
70. Sales Forecasting: A Practical & Proven Guide to Strategic Sales Forecasting
71. Elevate & Energize: *50 Dynamic & Fun Activities for Peak Workplace Morale*
72. 'Sales SOS! Sales on Fire! *30 Days to Conquer Chaos & the Nightmares of Success!'*
73. Mastering Sales Managerial Skills: *Building High-Performing Teams & Driving Exceptional Results*
74. Eagle-Eyed Leadership: Unleashing the Power of 31 Lessons from Eagles
75. The Ultimate Employee Training Guide: *Training Today, Leading Tomorrow*
76. Being More Accountable at Work
77. Creating a Culture of Continuous Improvement
78. Effective Questioning & Listening Skills
79. The Power of Value Selling
80. The Growth Mindset
81. Mastering Professional Help Desk Skills
82. The Power to Lead with Empathy
83. Being Prepared: The Key to Unlocking Success
84. Youthful Spark-Youth Energizers, Activities and Games-Igniting the Fun in Youth
85. Ignite your Motivation for Success
86. Elevate Your Executive Presence: *Your Roadmap to Executive Excellence*
87. Smart Decisions: *Mastering Problem Solving with Strategic Solutions for Business Success*
88. Strategic Planning: *Developing and Implementing Strategic Plans to Achieve Long-Term Business Goals*
89. The Power of Stay Interviews
90. Developing G.R.I.T.
91. Adaptability
92. Diagnosis- *A Key Skill for Leadership*
93. The Burnout-Proof Salesperson: *The Master Guide to Preventing Stress & Burnout-* Strategies for Thriving in Sales
94. Learning from Failure: *Keys to Success*
95. Customer Success Management
96. Overcoming the Killers of Motivation
97. The C-Suite Code: *Mastering Skills for Executive Excellence'*

98. Dealing with Difficult Customers
99. Unlocking Your Potential: Mastering the Top 20 Life Skills for a Brighter Future
100. Nurturing Tomorrow's Leaders: *Essential Soft Skills Every Child Must Learn*
101. Lively & Fun Party Games for Seniors & Elders
102. Role Playing for Sales Champions: From Practice to Performance
103. Fun and Exciting Party Games for Kids
104. Case Studies for Sales
105. Role-Playing for Unbeatable Customer Service
106. Case Studies in Customer Service
107. Case Studies in Winning Negotiations
108. Case Studies in Management & Leadership
109. Case Studies in Human Resources & Talent Management
110. CEO Success Blueprint: The Essential Toolkit for CEOs and C-Level Executives
111. The Salesperson's Self-Coaching Guide: *Master Your Own Self-Coaching Plan for Success*
112. Overcoming Procrastination: *Your Ultimate Guide to Stop Delaying and Start Living Your Best Life*
113. When True Colors Are Exposed: *The Journey to Unmasking Humanity*
114. Life-Changing Habits for Teens: Teen Success Blueprint for a Bright Future
115. Workplace Stress-Free: *Proven Strategies to Thrive at Work and Beyond*
116. Objection Overruled: *The Ultimate Guide to Turning 'No' into 'Yes'*
117. Building Strong Teams: *A Comprehensive Guide to Team Building*
118. Ethical & Moral Leadership in Business: *Eliminating Unethical Practices & Building a Culture of Trust & Integrity*
119. Rising Strong: Building Positive: High Self-Esteem for a Fulfilling Life-*A Practical Guide for Students, Employees, Leaders & Entrepreneurs*
120 The Cheerful Mindset: Cultivating a Joyful Outlook Everyday
121. Leading Through Crisis: Case Studies on Crisis Management

From the Ministry side, Gerard graduated in the very first batch of Charis Bible College-India & had for over 9 years served as a Part-time Faculty at Charis Bible College-Chennai (Andrew Wommack Ministries-Colorado, USA). He also holds a Diploma in Worship (a subject closest to his heart) from the JSOW and is also a graduate of the Advanced Mentorship Program (AMP) and the Circle Of Ministerial Engagement (C.O.M.E.) of Prophet Jerome Fernando and a Spiritual Son of the Esteemed Prophet. An accomplished author of several Secular & Christian Books, Gerard has been on the board of a few international organizations and boasts of being the SON of the MOST HIGH GOD: An ordinary guy following an extraordinary GOD!

...And some of his most recent Christian Books being:

1. A Bouquet of Praises for My KING
2. Christian Jokes for the Serious Religious' Folks!
3. Jesus Healed You!
4. Praise24Ever! (also in Tamil version)
5. The 5G Network of GOD
6. Building Faith over F.E.A.R- FACE EVERYTHING AND RISE with JESUS
7. Hebrew and Greek Praise and Worship Words
8. Godly Mothers' and Grandmothers' Bible Story time for Kids!
9. Miracles of Jesus in Pictures
10. Raise your Praise all 365 Days
11. Thanking GOD with an Attitude of Gratitude
12. Meditating on the Attributes of GOD
13. Puppet Scripts
14. Alcohol Ruins, JESUS Reforms, Renews & Restores!
15. Habakkuk 2:2 Christian Daily Journal, Planner & Organizer
16. ABC of GOD's Word for Handwriting Practice
17. Daily Bible Verse Handwriting Practice (Building Godly Character & Faith through Cursive Handwriting Practice!)
18. Guiding Light: Fun & Faith-Building Bible Activities for Children
19. Rejecting Grasshopper Talk: From Grasshopper to Giant-Killer-*Defeating Giants Daily!*
20. Teen Titans of Faith: *Building Courage, Determination & Christ-like-Esteem*
21. I AM Empowered: *Unleashing Divine Power with Positive*

Declarations

22. Be A Solution Provider-*From Passion to Purpose*: *A Biblical Guide to Being the Answer to the World!*
23. Miracles of JESUS
24. Parables of Jesus for a Meaningful Life!
25. A Grateful Heart: Importance of Sharing Testimonies of GOD's Grace
26. Melodies of Worship to JESUS: 31 Songs of Praise & Worship From My Heart to HIS!
27. I AM SO BLESSED!
28. My Daily Cup of Energizer
29. 31 Leadership Lessons *from* Jesus- *The Supreme Leader*
30. Peace Amidst Storms: A Biblical Guide to Conquering S.T.R.E.S.S.
31. Rise Above: 20 Biblical Eagle Lessons for Life's Triumphs
32. Godly Goal Setting: *The FAITHFUL Blueprint for a Purpose-Driven Life*
33. The Profound Attributes of our Mighty GOD: Understanding the 10S's of the Almighty
34. Worship Now, Worship Forever: *A Journey from Earthly Praise to Eternal Glory*
35. Unceasing Praise & Worship: *365 Days to Worship the King*
36. The ROAR Within: *Living with Purpose and Authority through the Power of the Holy Spirit*
37. From Potential to Purpose: Unlocking and Multiplying Your Talents & Gifts for Kingdom Impact
38. Songs from the Heart: *Worshipping GOD in Your Own Tune & Melody*
39. Awakening Praise & Worship: Hebrew & Greek Words to Raise Your Praise
40. Sing a NEW Song to the LORD Everyday: *Daily Devotions of Praise & Worship to Lift Your Heart & Glorify HIS Name*
41. *The* A.R.O.M.A. of True Worship: *Creating Worship That Delights God*
42. Becoming A Kingdom Champion: *Embracing God's Call for a Life of Purpose & Victory*
43. The Busy Businessman's Daily Devotional: 366 Crisp Truths to Start Your Day Strong
44. The Teacher's Heart: *Daily Devotions for Educators*
45. Anchored! *A 31-Day Devotional for Students Facing Life's Challenges*
46. Suddenly! Unlocking Unorthodox Breakthroughs through Unusual Worship

47. Overcoming Adversity: *Lessons from the Bible for Modern Challenges*
48. LORD, Don't do it without me
49. Kingdom Leadership: *Biblical Principles for Modern Leaders*
50. Heartprints of God- *Growing God's Way:* Daily Devotions for Kids to Shine Bright
51. Send Judah First: Let your Praises Go up First to See the Mighty Move of GOD
52. DIVINE MOMENTS: *Recognizing, Embracing, Preparing, and Walking into Life-Changing Encounters with God*
53. Be a Builder in the Kingdom: *The C.E.M.E.N.T. Guide to Creating a Lasting Legacy*
54. Unshakable: *Pillars of Godly Womanhood* (Pillars of Faith That Changed History)
55. Lead Like a Shepherd: *14 Essential Traits for Pastoral Excellence*
56. The Worship Leader's Arsenal: *Powerful Exhortations to Ignite Thanksgiving, Praise & Worship*
57. Women of UnShakable Faith: *31-Day Devotional for Strength, Purpose & Influence*
58. Called to Teach: *A Complete 10-Week Training Guide for Impactful VBS Teachers*
59. Strumming for the KING: Cowboy Songs of Faith & Fire
60. The Ultimate Youth Camp Playbook: *50 Bible-Centered Indoor Games to Engage, Equip, and Empower Teens*
61. Glad in HIS Presence: *David's Revelation of GOD's Love & Mercy*
62. The Spirit Behind the Sound: *52 Devotionals for Worship Teams*
63. THE COWBOY'S COMPASS: *Riding the Trail of Faith with Grit & Grace*
64. Worship as My Weapon: *Living Victoriously through the Power of Praise*
65. A Worshipper Always Wins*: Living a Life of Victorious Worship*
66. Worship That Leads to the Throne: *Practical Strategies for Worship Leaders to Inspire Their Team & Usher People into God's Presence*
67. Worship as Warfare: *Conquering through the Sound of Surrender*
68. Watchmen on the Walls: *A 31-Day Devotional for Worship Teams*

69. KINGDOM BUSINESS: *52 Biblical Principles for GODLY Leadership & Wise Decisions*
70. From Evening to Morning: *Rediscovering GOD's Sacred Hours*
71. Waves of Glory: *Worship through Dance, Flags, Staff & Sound*
72. WORSHIP TEAM BUILDER: *Guiding Your Team from Formation to Fruitfulness*
73. The Worship Leader's Master Training Manual
74. Skits for the King: Children's Plays for Every Church Occasion
75. Unbreakable: Building Strong Marriages and Families God's Way *(From Vows to Victory)*
76. Songs for my King: *A 31-Day Journey of Praise*
77. Building Powerful Children: *Raising a Generation That Will Shape the Future for God*
78. Character Before Chords: *The Heart of the True Worshipper*

Besides regularly contributing to business & trade journals, including international ones such as the 'Creative Training Techniques' and the 'Sales News' of the U.S.A, He is also a member of several prestigious bodies & trade associations, having participated in many Conferences & Workshops in India & Overseas.

Prior to his last assignment of leading & managing a large MNC as head, Gerard had a 3-year stint in the Middle East as a Consultant with a leading British Consultancy Firm.

As the past 'Official Country Representative' for the International Business Award- 'THE STEVIES'-(the business world's own Oscar) for about 4 years- he ensured a few Indian companies that qualify for the same every year!

Gerard can be contacted at:
Email: training@Sales-Training.in,training@CollectionSkills.com
Websites:

www.Sales-Training.in
www.EtiquetteWorks.in
www.CollectionSkills.com
www.RetailSalesTraining.in
www.SalesTrainingIndia.com
www.ManualPreparation.com
www.TrainingWithPuppets.com
www.FirstContactAcademy.com
www.SalesAndMarketingRecruiter.com

www.ingramcontent.com/pod-product-compliance
Ingram Content Group UK Ltd.
Pitfield, Milton Keynes, MK11 3LW, UK
UKHW021340190726
13845UKWH00027B/650

9 788199 301795